Perennials
for the
Plains and
Prairies

Edgar wishes to dedicate this labor of love to his deceased parents Frederick Wesley Toop and Pearl Edith (Simpson) Toop who instilled in him a love of horticulture.

Sara wishes to make her dedication to her mother, Dora Rabinovitz.

Canadian Cataloguing in Publication Data
    Toop, Ed, 1932–
        Perennials for the Plains and Prairies

    Previous ed. has title: Perennials for the Prairies.

    ISBN: 1-55001-029-9

    1. Perennials – Prairie Provinces. 2. Perennials – Great Plains.
I. Williams, Sara, 1941- .   II. University of Alberta. Faculty
of Extension.   III. Title.   IV. Title: Perennials for the Prairies.

SB434.T66 1997   635.9'32'09712   C97-910711-3

The Production Team

Managing Editors:	Thom Shaw
	C Val Smyth
Page Composition:	Lu Ziola
Page Design and Layout:	Melanie Eastley
Illustrations:	Melanie Eastley
	Rusty Brown
Copy Editor:	Lois Hameister
Technical Reviewers:	Lynn Collicutt
	Allan Daku
	Gillian Ford
	Patrick Healey
Cover Photographs:	Tom Shaw
	Alberta Agriculture, Food and Rural Development

Preface

Prairie gardeners are generally overlooked by the majority of gardening books which are written for the more temperate areas of the continent with a longer growing season in which a greater variety of plants can be grown easily. This book deals specifically with perennial flowers that are hardy enough to survive our long cold winters. Survival involves more than an inherent tolerance to freezing temperatures. The fluctuating nature of the continental prairie climate necessitates protection from drying winds, shading from the penetrating rays of the late winter sun and the trapping of snow for insulation of all but a few rugged, often indigenous, plant species. Despite these restrictions, with good planning and attention to the specific needs of each plant, a rather impressive array of perennial flowers can be grown successfully .

As the name implies, perennial plants tend to persist for a number of years, provided of course, they are given a bit of encouragement. Not all perennial flowering plants are desirable (some of our peskiest weeds are perennials), nor are they all successful in the prairie environment. However, there are more perennials that fit the criteria of desirability and hardiness than possibly can be dealt with in one book. Choices for inclusion in this book are based on experimental research, the experience of the authors, to some extent their biases, and on suggestions from colleagues.

The vast array of attractive herbaceous perennials with their wide range of flowering periods, running the full growing season from the end of winter until winter sets in again, permits the design of flower beds that are attractive, interesting and ever changing. Perennials are indeed a versatile group that provides more than just a brilliant splash of color during the summer.

Ed Toop
Sara Williams

Foreword

Even in gardening, fashions change—and I have been pleased to notice among gardeners of the plains and prairies an increasing interest in those old fashioned plants, herbaceous perennials. Perennials have always enjoyed a certain amount of popularity and many a prairie garden has a prized peony, old-fashioned iris or group of sweet-smelling lily-of-the-valley, usually inherited from a relative or a generous neighbor.

For many years the Devonian Botanic Garden has been growing a wide range of hardy herbaceous perennials and trying to convince others to do the same. With the realization that these plants are indeed hardy and easy to grow and with the ever improving selection of new cultivars, we get a great number of inquiries about them. Now, here is a book that I can recommend to both the beginner and the more advanced gardener. It covers approximately 200 perennials: from fussy plants for the alpine garden to easy space fillers for the back lane; from old favorites to new and exciting cultivars; all with descriptions of color, height and suggested use, plus practical cultural instructions. Photographs and line drawings supplement those intimidating but necessary Latin names making this a decidedly "user friendly" book.

Although herbaceous perennials are ideally suited to the prairie garden—particularly one with a good snow cover— not all are equally hardy. A copy of this book in your gardening library will not only encourage you to try something new, but will save you both time and money.

Gillian Ford
Assistant director
Devonian Botanic Garden

About the authors

Edgar Toop is a graduate of Ohio State University, having received his Master of Science in 1957 (Floriculture) and Doctorate in 1960 (Plant Pathology). After completion of his formal education he taught general botany at Ohio State University before going to the University of Alberta, Canada, as a horticulture professor. He is currently a professor emeritus from the University of Alberta, having retired in 1987 after 25 years of service to its Faculty of Agriculture, Forestry and Home Economics.

Over the years, he has served on the executive of various agricultural and horticultural organizations including the Canadian Society for Horticultural Science and the Western Canadian Society for Horticulture, an organization that included members from the Great Plains States and Alaska. He is a member of both the International Society for Horticultural Science and the Sigma Xi.

Edgar was recognized by the Alberta Horticultural Association in 1987 when he was awarded the Centennial Gold Medal (the Association's highest award for horticultural achievement). In 1990 he was the recipient of the Alberta Greenhouse Growers Association's Meritorious Service Award. He has also been awarded an honorary life membership in the Western Canadian Society for Horticulture and the Canadian Society for Horticultural Science.

Sara Williams received her BA in History and English from the University of Michigan in 1963. She taught overseas as a Peace Corps volunteer in Tanzania and later in Peru. Originally from the United States, she immigrated to Canada in 1972.

In 1987, she received her Bachelor of Science in Agriculture, with Great Distinction, from the University of Saskatchewan, majoring in Horticultural Extension. She was awarded the Gold Medal by the Western Canadian Society for Horticulture in 1987, and the Distinguished Extension Award by the Canadian Society of Extension in 1989. She received her Master of Science in 1997 in Agricultural Extension.

Sara is a Horticulture Specialist with the Extension Division, University of Saskatchewan. She is also the author of *Commercial Saskatoon Berry Production on the Prairies, Commercial Raspberry Production on the Prairies,* and editor of the quarterly magazine *The Saskatchewan Gardener.* Her most recent book (1997) is *Creating the Prairie Xeriscape, low input, low maintenance gardening.* She does regular radio gardening shows and leads garden tours to Europe.

She grows few annuals, but admits to having occasionally been given geraniums by well-meaning friends.

Acknowledgements

The authors wish to thank their colleagues who have encouraged them in the writing of this book. Particular thanks go to: Lynn Collicutt, horticultural research scientist at the Agriculture Canada Research Station, Morden, Manitoba; Gillian Ford, assistant director of the University of Alberta Devonian Botanic Garden, Edmonton, Alberta; Patrick Healey, owner/operator of Oakhill Farm, Belmont, Manitoba; and Allan Daku owner/operator of Honeywood Lilies, Parkside, Saskatchewan, for their generous constructive criticism as technical reviewers.

Thanks are also extended to Donna Balzer, horticulturist with the Calgary Zoological Society for data made available on tulip trials held at the Dorothy Harvie Gardens in Calgary. We also wish to acknowledge the use of unpublished information compiled by the late Dr C F Patterson, the first head of the Department of Horticulture at the University of Saskatchewan in Saskatoon.

Thanks are also extended to the institutions and many individuals who contributed photographic materials. We are indebted to: Olds College, Olds, Alberta; University of Alberta Department of Plant Science, Edmonton; the Saskatchewan Department of Agriculture and Food; the Alberta Horticultural Association; Agriculture and Agri-food Canada, Morden; Gail Rankin, Edmonton; Hugh Knowles, Edmonton; Brian Porter, Regina; Gabe Botar, Edmonton; Anita Schill, Olds; W.E. Smith, Alberta; and Bill Andrew, Edmonton.

We have greatly appreciated the innovative talent and sincere dedication of the production team that made this book possible.

Table of Contents

How to use this book

The opening four chapters of *Perennials for the Plains and Prairies* deal with the general aspects of propagation, culture and use of hardy herbaceous perennials in the home landscape. The fifth chapter deals specifically with hardy bulbs and includes descriptions of those kinds recommended for the prairie regions of North America.

The second section of the book includes an alphabetical listing of what we might call regular perennials (excluding bulbs) giving descriptive details and specific hints on propagation, culture and use. At the end of this section is a **master reference chart** which summarizes the pertinent information, including short comings, about the individual plants or groups of closely related plants dealt with in the book. This reference chart serves also as an **index**.

Color plates and **illustrative drawings** occur throughout the book to enhance the printed word.

We have attempted to avoid technical terms throughout the text but have included a glossary for those words which may be unfamiliar to the reader.

Harbingers

of the

Season

INTRODUCTION

A **herbaceous perennial** can be defined as a non-woody ornamental plant that dies back or is killed back to ground level each winter, but produces new top growth each spring. It normally lives at least three years under local conditions, but may live a human lifetime, or longer. However, it may also act as a biennial or even an annual in a situation in which it is not at home. A **biennial** is defined as a plant that starts from seed, produces a leafy plant the first year, produces flowers and seeds the second growing season, and then dies. An annual, on the other hand, produces a leafy plant, flowers, and seed in a single growing season, and then dies. Many of the so-called annual flowers that we grow in our gardens are in fact tender herbaceous perennials that are unable to survive as perennials in our climate. In order for a plant to be used as a perennial in our gardens it must be hardy. Hardiness of any plant is primarily based on its successful adaptation to cold, although other climatic factors have a bearing as well. Plant hardiness also involves tolerance of drought, soil conditions, debilitating heat, excessive wind, and changes in light intensity and duration.

FIGURE 1.

Bergenia cordifolia
(giant rockfoil)

FIGURE 2.

Iberis sempervirens
(perennial candytuft)

FIGURE 3.

Lythrum
(loosestrife)

Like all concise definitions, the above definition of a hardy herbaceous perennial does not take into account the complete spectrum of all the plants included in this book. There are plants such as giant rockfoil and perennial candytuft that are evergreen in habit. The leaves may wilt and turn purple, brown, or black with the cold, but will be resurrected to their normal color and function in the spring. Furthermore, some of the plants we have included, such as loosestrife, develop rather woody stems by the end of the summer. However, these stocks are easily pruned back to ground level at the end of the growing season.

Some perennials, including hardy types, develop a well defined storage organ below ground. This may be in the form of a **tuberous root**, a **bulb**, a **corm**, a **tuber**, or a thick fleshy **rhizome**. Although these plants are truly herbaceous perennials, they are often treated separately in the literature. We have chosen to do the same by dealing with hardy "bulbs" in Chapter 5.

As a group, the hardy herbaceous perennials are truly harbingers of all the seasons. With careful planning and judicious choice of species and varieties they can provide an ongoing parade of changing colors and textures from the time the snow banks start receding in early spring until winter returns with a fresh mantle of snow. Furthermore, they give repeat performances, each a little different from the one before.

HISTORY OF HERBACEOUS BORDERS

Evidence for the planting of flowers in beds or borders goes back to ancient times but the history of the herbaceous border as a separate feature is short. In ancient Persia the love of flowers induced people to grow them in beds along walkways. But it is from the chronicles of medieval times that we read of physic gardens at monasteries, neatly laid out in beds bordered by beds of flowers. The growing of various herbs, particularly for medicinal purposes, was an important aspect of the times. Although no reference was made to herbaceous plants as such, it is fairly certain that the flowers referred to would have been herbaceous perennials for the most part in a garden of this nature.

Phillip Miller's *Dictionary of Gardening* which appeared in 1724 describes what can only be a true herbaceous border. "Gardeners are making borders along the sidewalks for their choicest flowers and …where flowers are desired, there may be borders continued round the extent of the lawn, immediately before the plantation of shrubs, which if properly planted with hardy flowers to succeed each other will afford a more pleasing prospect." (taken from *Guide to Hardy Perennials* by Frances Perry). However, it was not until 1890 that the phrase "hardy herbaceous perennials" with reference to a flower border was coined. George Nicolson, at that time the eminent curator of the Royal Botanic Gardens, Kew, is credited with using the term first. However, Nicolson only started the idea for this type of gardening using herbaceous perennials exclusively. Most of the credit for the rapid popularity of this concept should go to Miss Gertrude Jekyll and William Robinson, two great plants people of the 19th century. Robinson remarks in *The English Flower Garden*, "The true way to make gardens yield a return of beauty for the labour and skill given them is the permanent one … let the beds be planted as permanently and as well as possible, so that there will remain little to do for years." To achieve that goal he stressed the importance of judicious choice of kinds stating, "Select only good plants, throw away weedy kinds, there is no scarcity of the best."

FIGURE 4.
Delphiniums

Ed Toop

FIGURE 5.
Island bed.

Lynn Collicutt

FIGURE 6.
Rock garden.

Alberta Horticultural Association

Propagating

Perennials

There are basically four methods for propagating perennials – from seed, from cuttings, by separation and division, and by layering.

STARTING PLANTS FROM SEED

Many herbaceous perennials are readily propagated from seed. This is often the cheapest method of obtaining new plants, especially in large quantities. However, not all plants can be propagated from seed. Many selections or named cultivars do not come true from seed but rather produce a mixture of off-type individuals most of which are likely to be inferior in appearance to the parent plant. If the plant in question is a **hybrid** that has been produced by crossing two selected parental lines, it can be propagated from seed, but only from seed produced from the controlled crossing of the parental lines. Many hybrids can only be propagated by vegetative means. If you are purchasing seeds, choose a reputable dealer to ensure that the seed is true to type, viable and free of weed seeds. If you are collecting seed, choose strong vigorous plants for harvesting.

DIRECT SEEDING

To start perennials from seed, plant the seed in rows in the garden in the spring. It usually takes two years to get flower production from seed so there is little to be gained by starting the seedlings indoors or in greenhouses. However, with smaller or more expensive seeds it might be worthwhile to sow the seed

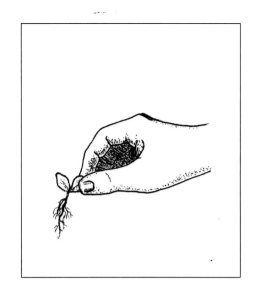

FIGURE 7.

Handling seedlings.

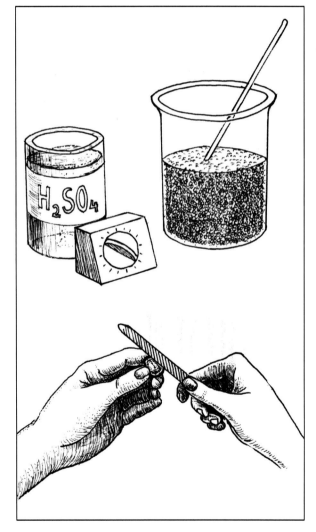

FIGURE 8.

Scarification. (A) acid treatment; (B) scratching seed coat.

indoors under lights. This gives the gardener more control over environmental factors. Although some kinds will produce a few flowers by late summer or fall, none will reach mature size and peak production until the second or third year. Once the seedlings are large enough to recognize and handle, thin or prick them out to allow individuals to develop into strong healthy plants by the end of the growing season. Although perennials vary in mature size, a spacing of approximately 10 to 15 cm (4 to 6 in.) is adequate the first season. By autumn many plants are an ideal size for transplanting to beds or borders.

From a convenience or maintenance standpoint, you may want to do the seeding, transplanting and growing in trays or pots rather than in the open garden. You can keep a closer watch on the seedlings and eliminate the need for thinning and even weeding. However, more frequent watering and fertilizing is necessary and two or more transplantings may be required in place of thinning.

SPECIAL TREATMENTS

Seeds of some kinds of perennials are **dormant**, which means they require special treatment before they will germinate. This dormancy is caused by various factors or combinations of factors. One common cause is a hard, impervious seed coat. Such seeds must have the coat cracked open or eroded away by mechanical, chemical or biological agents so that water and air can enter the seed to initiate growth processes. A second cause for dormancy is seed immaturity. Seeds of some plants are shed before the **embryo** is fully developed. A sequence of specific temperature changes is usually required to trigger this maturation or after-ripening process. A third cause for seed dormancy is the presence of growth suppressing compounds in the seed and/or the absence of growth promoters. Manipulation of temperature and moisture conditions provides the key for unlocking this form of dormancy.

Scarification

Scarification is the term used to describe the breaking or softening of hard seed coats. This is done by scarring individual seeds with a sharp file, rubbing the seed between two sheets of sandpaper, or tumbling seeds in a container with an abrasive agent such as carborundum. A short exposure of seeds to concentrated sulphuric or hydrochloric acid is a common chemical scarification treatment.

Stratification
    To hasten the breaking of internal dormancy, seeds are alternately layered (hence the term **stratification**) with a moist medium such as clean sand, sand-peat mixture, or peat. Temperature control (level and duration) provides the necessary treatment to break the internal dormancy of the stratified seed.

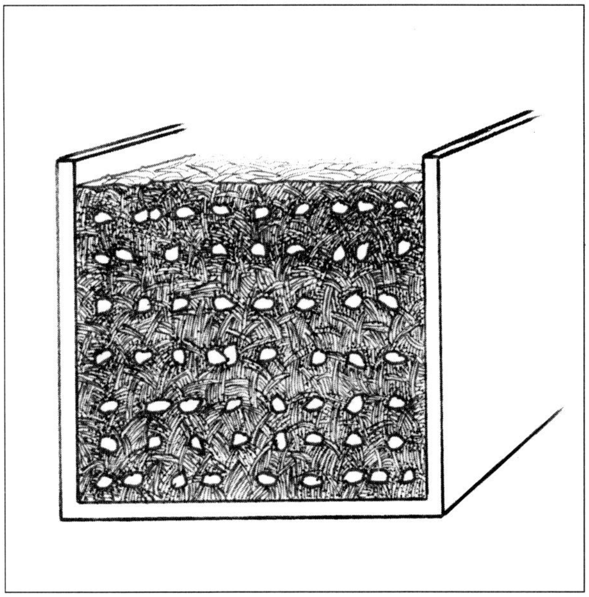

FIGURE 9.

Stratification.

STARTING PLANTS FROM CUTTINGS
    When plants do not "come true" from seeds, as in the case of hybrids, some means of vegetative reproduction should be used. This utilizes a plant part other than seeds. Cuttings may consist of portions of stems, entire leaves, or portions of leaves, a leaf plus the node of the stem to which it is attached or portions of roots. The size of cuttings and the age or maturity of the plant organs used for cuttings vary with the kind of plant being propagated and the amount of material available for use.

TERMINAL STEM CUTTINGS
    Terminal stem cuttings or "slips" are an easy way to start new plants. Once roots develop at or near the cut surface of the cuttings you have new complete plants. Such cuttings can be made from new growth in the spring and work well for species with rather woody stems such as chrysanthemum, summer phlox, and loosestrife. Cuttings of 8 to 10 cm (3 to 4 in.) in length can be removed when the shoots are about 15 cm (6 in.) high. Make the cuts at, or just below, a node, remove the bottom leaves, and stick the cuttings in a suitable medium in flats or pots. Sand-peat or perlite-peat mixes are commonly used for rooting. Plant crowns can be dug from the garden in late winter or early spring and brought into a greenhouse to induce early growth for cuttings. It is also possible to cut down mature plants after they have

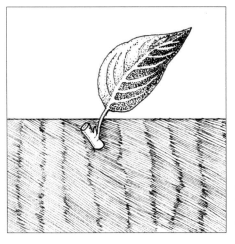

FIGURE 10.

Terminal stem cuttings.

FIGURE 11.

Leaf- bud cuttings.

flowered in the summer to induce new shoots for use as cuttings.

LEAF-BUD CUTTINGS

Leaf-bud cuttings are handled in a similar fashion to stem cuttings but consist of only a short piece of stem with a leaf attached. Leaves are attached to stems only at nodes, and in the axils of those leaves will be one or more buds. These buds may or may not be visible. Once such a cutting roots and the bud develops into a shoot, a new complete plant has been created. It takes longer to get a good sized plant

FIGURE 12.

Root cuttings.

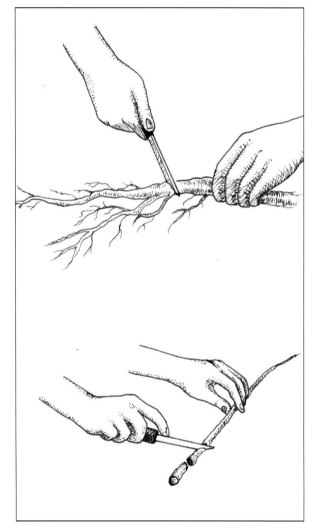

from a leaf-bud cutting than from a stem cutting, but many more plants can be produced from the same amount of cutting material. If a plant has opposite leaf arrangement (two leaves at a node), you can make two cuttings from each node by cutting through the centre of the stem segment. Leaf-bud cuttings work best, however, on plants with fairly thick or sturdy stems.

LEAF CUTTINGS

Leaf cuttings involve an entire leaf (blade and petiole), the blade only, or a portion of the blade. Leaf cuttings are popular for propagating African violets, begonias, and other house plants. For leaf cuttings to be successful not only do roots have to be initiated but a bud must form as well. Not all plants have the genetic capability for initiating buds in tissues other than that at stem nodes. Although leaf cuttings from such plants may develop roots and remain healthy and alive, they remain just that, healthy rooted leaves. For this reason, leaf cuttings are not generally recommended for propagating herbaceous perennials.

ROOT CUTTINGS

Root cuttings, on the other hand, are useful for propagating many plants, particularly those with rather thick or vigorous root systems, such as *Anchusa, Dicentra, Echinops, Gaillardia, Gysophila* and *Limonium*. Dig up stock plants in the fall before freeze-up or in late winter or early spring before new growth starts. Select straight healthy roots 5 to 7 mm (0.2 to 0.3 in.) in diameter and cut these into segments 3 to 5 cm (1.2 to 2 in.) long. Plant the segments horizontally or at an oblique angle 15 to 30 mm (0.6 to 1.2 in.) deep in cold frames or flats containing a suitable soil mix or rooting medium. If you are fall planting, store the flats in cold frames at 10°C (50°F) over winter and insulate cold frames with a mulch of leaves or dry peat. When exposed to growing temperatures in the spring, buds will develop and produce shoots and a functional root

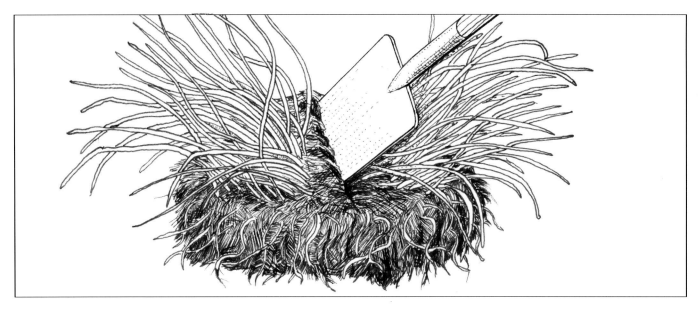

system will develop underground. Plants are ready for transplanting when top growth is 8 to 10 cm (3 to 4 in.) tall. Cuttings made at the end of the winter, rather than in the fall, will also develop new plants in the spring.

PROPAGATION BY SEPARATION AND DIVISION

In addition to using seeds or cuttings, many perennials can be propagated by **separation** or **division** .

SEPARATION

Plants that develop bulbs or similar storage organs underground usually multiply these structures in a dense circle of increasing diameter. If you dig up such plants and separate the individual bulbs, tubers, or tuberous roots, you can replant these structures and grow a new independent plant from each one.

DIVISION

Although only a limited number of perennial flowers produce such well defined storage organs, most do develop a good sized crown composed of food laden buds at or near the soil surface. It is these buds that give rise to the new top growth each spring. Much of the crown of vigorous plants must be discarded every three or four years to keep them in check. Others such as peonies, for example, can remain undisturbed for 10 or more years without ever expanding beyond a diameter of attractive proportions.

To obtain more plants, dig up the crown, chop it into clumps of convenient size, and replant the individual clumps. Because the center of the crown has often died out or is less vigorous than the outer band, choose the most vigorous outer portions for replanting.

FIGURE 13.

Separation of crowns.

FIGURE 14.

Division and replanting of crowns.

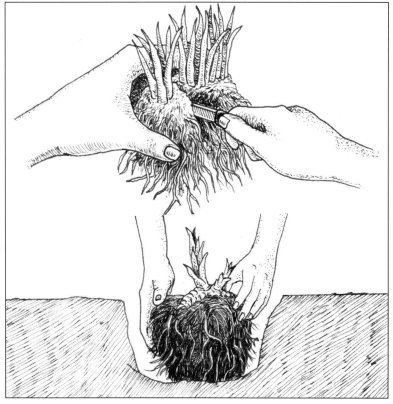

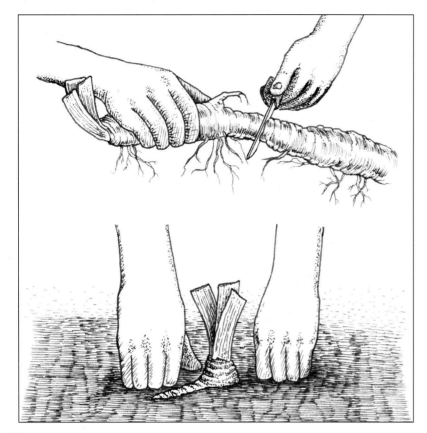

FIGURE 15. Division and replanting of rhizomes.

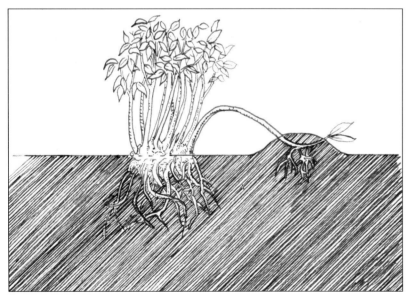

FIGURE 16. Simple layering.

For rejuvenation or for propagation purposes, divide crowns in the spring when the ground is workable and new growth is starting. However, for early flowering plants, wait until right after flowering. A few kinds are best divided at a specific time during the growing season that is not directly related to time of flowering. For example, it is recommended that bearded iris be divided or transplanted in July or early August, Oriental poppies about mid-August and peonies in early September.

PROPAGATION BY LAYERING

Layering is another method for propagating perennials. Many prostrate plants used as ground covers tend to root naturally along the stems that are in contact with the ground. This is natural layering and occurs with such plants as *Arabis* and *Thymus*. The deliberate layering of stems by pinning them down to the soil or partially burying them is successful with many plants.

Simple layering, tip layering and mound layering are three slightly different techniques that have proved successful with certain perennial flowers.

SIMPLE LAYERING

Simple layering involves the bending down of a well developed shoot or stem and burying a short segment of the stem in soil back several centimetres from the apex or tip. To hasten the formation of roots, partially cut through the underside of the stem at the point where it is to be buried. Use a wire staple or weight of some kind to keep the stem pinned down.

TIP LAYERING

Tip layering differs from simple layering in that the stem apex is buried. As the apex continues to grow it emerges from the soil and roots form where the stem remains buried.

MOUND LAYERING

Mound layering involves the mounding of additional soil over the crown of the plant thus burying the base of the existing stems to a depth of approximately 8 cm (3 in.). After **adventitious** roots have formed on the base of these shoots, carefully remove the soil and cut off the shoots at crown level. Layering involves the rooting of stems before cuttings are made. It is used on plants that root very slowly from traditional stem cuttings.

BUYING STARTED PLANTS

With the increased interest in herbaceous perennials in recent years, a greater selection of species and cultivars is available in the market place. Many greenhouse and nursery growers are starting herbaceous perennials as a part of their diversified crop production and many garden centers have a good selection available in the spring.

Deal with a reputable firm and check the plants for any evidence of disease or insect damage or infestation. Container-grown plants should have a well developed root system and can be transplanted to the garden almost any time during the growing season. Depending on supply and demand, they may be available for purchase from spring through fall.

FIGURE 17.

Mound layering.

FIGURE 18.

Nursery/bedding plants.

Cultivating

Perennials

In order for perennials to grow and thrive, the soil must contain the essential elements and be at an optimum pH. Temperature, moisture, and light conditions must also be favorable. Finally, any planting or transplanting needs to take place at certain times in the growing season.

SOIL FOR PERENNIALS

Any good garden soil will grow perennials. Proper preparation of the soil prior to planting ensures that the plants develop strong root systems, a prerequisite for maximum flower development. A medium garden loam of good tilth is ideal, but almost any soil can be modified to approach this ideal. For example, a very sandy soil can be made into loamy soil by the incorporation of peat, compost or well rotted manure. This **organic matter** increases the water holding capacity of the soil, helps bind the sand together, and yet maintains excellent drainage. Oddly enough, a soil high in clay can have its tilth greatly improved with the same treatment. In this instance the organic matter dilutes the clay keeping it from compacting and becoming sticky thus improving both the drainage and the aeration. Clay soils may also benefit from the incorporation of coarse or large-grained sand as well as organic matter to help stabilize a good soil structure. However, clay plus sand is also a good recipe for "concrete" so care

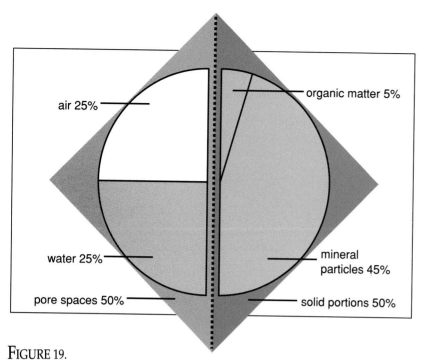

FIGURE 19.

Components of soil.

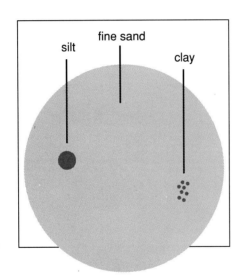

FIGURE 20.

Relative size of soil/mineral particles.

must be taken in amending heavy, clay soils. It is this tilth or soil structure that is of utmost importance since there must be both air and water surrounding the roots in the soil if the roots are to remain alive and continue to grow and function.

ESSENTIAL ELEMENTS

Most of the nutrients required by plants are absorbed through their root systems. Therefore it is essential that these materials be present in the soil in adequate amounts. All sixteen **essential elements** for plant growth are usually present in soil but not always in optimum quantities. Of the sixteen, six are required in relatively large amounts. These **macronutrients** are nitrogen, phosphorus, potassium, calcium, magnesium and sulfur. Of this group nitrogen, phosphorus and potassium are the three most likely to become short in supply and need to be added regularly as fertilizer.

It is the balance of nitrogen, phosphorus and potassium (N, P and K) available to plants that regulates the growth and development of a plant, provided all other factors essential to plant growth are in place. Nitrogen encourages vegetative or leafy development and is particularly important in the early part of the growing season. However, if nitrogen is available in large quantities in relation to phosphorus and potassium, it can delay flowering and restrict root growth. Phosphorus is particularly important for healthy root growth and both phosphorus and potassium are important in flowering and fruiting. This is why a complete fertilizer (10-30-10, 20-20-20, or 5-10-5) is recommended for gardens rather than a lawn fertilizer which is high in nitrogen (the first number) and low in phosphorus and/or potassium. Some prairie soils are naturally high in potassium and may require N-P fertilizer only (16-20-0 or 11-48-0).

SOIL pH

For plants to be healthy and productive not only must all the essential elements be present in the soil but they must also be available to the roots. To be available they must be in a soluble ionic form. This explains why the **pH** or degree of **acidity** or **alkalinity** of a soil is so closely tied to soil fertility. Each nutrient is soluble over a range of pH but will be most soluble at a specific pH reading. The best average pH reading for ensuring that all the essential elements will be soluble is about 6.2. Therefore, for most herbaceous perennials the ideal pH range for the soil is 6.0 to 6.5 which is slightly acidic (7.0 is neutral). Acid-loving plants such as azalea or blueberry for instance will grow best at pHs below 6.0 whereas other plants such as perennial sweet peas will do best at a pH near 7.5. These plants vary from the norm because of their high demand for a specific element such as iron or calcium which reaches its peak of solubility outside the 6.0 to 6.5 range.

Although regular incorporation of compost or well rotted manure will usually maintain an adequate balance of nutrients for perennials, many will perform better if given supplementary applications of chemical fertilizers. To determine the amount of fertilizer to add and how often, have your soil tested. Soil testing is provided by both commercial and government laboratories for a fee. You will receive recommendations for bringing the soil fertility into balance for the plants you intend to grow.

Be careful when you purchase top soil or manures for use in the home garden. Some topsoils have been treated with a non- or slowly-degradable herbicide to eliminate weeds before the top soil is removed for sale. This treated topsoil is toxic to most plants grown in it afterward. Also be aware that animal wastes can concentrate certain pesticide residues present on the feed consumed by the animals. This in turn can cause toxicity symptoms on plants whose roots come in contact with these toxins. Ask questions about the quality of the products. Get some sort of insurance in writing if you have any suspicions about the integrity of the product.

TEMPERATURE AND MOISTURE

Soil temperature and moisture also influence plant growth. A properly prepared soil with good structure should have good drainage, but if the top soil is shallow and the subsoil is compacted or rather impervious to water, drainage tiles may have to be installed to ensure proper drainage. To do this, lay tiles made of fired clay, concrete or plastic, or possibly perforated pipe, underground at about 45 to 60 cm (18 to 24 in.) in depth in lines spaced about 60 to 100 cm (2 to 3 ft.) apart.

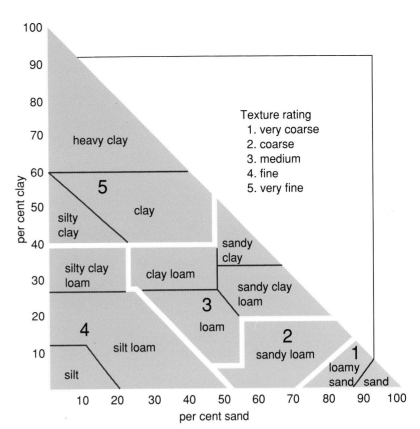

FIGURE 21. Texture triangle.

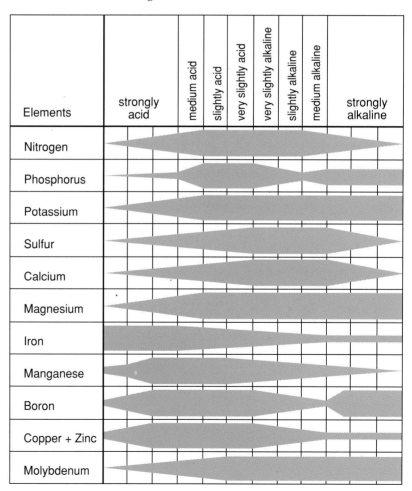

FIGURE 22. Solubility of nutrients at various pH levels.

FIGURE 23.

Drainage system installation.

FIGURE 24.

Staking plants.

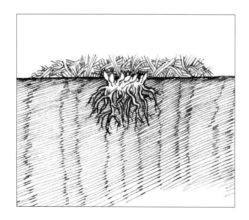

FIGURE 25.

Mulching.

These lines should slope very slightly toward the outlet at a pitch of about 8 cm per 15 m (3 in. per 15 yd.). Good drainage ensures that the soil warms up quickly in the spring. Soil may be mounded into raised beds of up to 30 to 60 cm (1 to 2 ft.) depth as an alternative method to the installation of drainage tile

WIND PROTECTION

Protection from wind is also important in preventing moisture loss from soil which, in turn, affects soil temperature. The perennials themselves will provide wind protection during the growing season. To ensure year-round protection, provide wind breaks in the form of shrubs, trees or man-made structures. If trees or shrubs are used, species which have tap root or limited fibrous root systems should be chosen so that competition for moisture and nutrients between these woody plants and the herbaceous perennials is minimized.

MULCHING

Covering the soil surface with either plastic or organic mulches is another way of conserving soil moisture and controlling soil temperature. Plastic will trap solar energy and warm the soil, which is ideal for warm season crops such as melons and cucumbers. However, most perennials prefer a cool but moist soil. That is what makes organic mulches ideal since they insulate the soil surface from the hot sun yet reduce evaporation of water. Mulching will also reduce mud splash, cushion the soil against compaction, and prevent crusting of the soil surface, a condition that hinders the percolation of rain and irrigation water down into the soil. An organic mulch also gradually decays adding to the organic content of the soil. The organisms that bring about this decay release nutrients in the organic matter making them available to the plant roots. Leaf litter, straw, ground corn cobs, wood chips and many other materials can be used as a mulch but coarse peat moss is most commonly used. A depth of 7.5 to 10 cm (3 to 4 in.) is adequate.

WATERING

Seldom is the natural precipitation adequate to maintain a flower bed at its peak of perfection throughout the growing season. It is important to monitor the soil moisture level regularly and apply irrigation when required. To determine soil moisture, dig down into the soil to a depth of about 15 to 30 cm (6 to 12 in.), take a handful of soil and squeeze it into a ball. If upon releasing the hand pressure, the ball falls apart, the moisture content is too low; if it stays closely packed together it is too wet; and if it partially breaks apart the moisture content is ideal. Soils of different texture (varying proportions of sand, silt and clay) react somewhat differently in this test but experience will improve your ability to interpret this test for different soils. If irrigation is necessary, add sufficient water to ensure that it penetrates deep into the root zone. The amount of water required depends upon the soil texture and the organic matter content. Clay particles and humus can absorb copious amounts of water in comparison to sand and silt. Avoid frequent but sparse watering which encourages shallow rooting rather than deep and extensive rooting thus making the plants much more susceptible to drought. It cannot be over emphasized that deep watering will encourage deep rooting which makes plants much more resistant to the stresses of heat, cold, and drought.

If you use rain water for irrigation, discard the initial runoff when rain occurs after an extended dry spell. After many weeks without rain, there may be significant air pollutant fallout on the roofs of buildings that could be concentrated enough in the initial runoff to be toxic to plants.

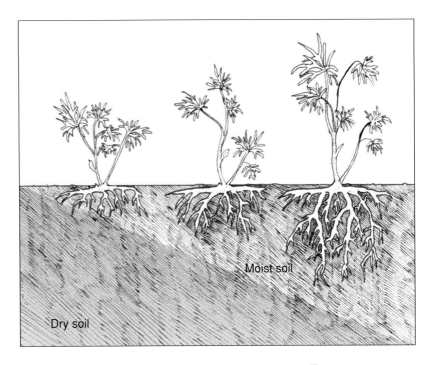

FIGURE 26.

Root and top growth development at different depths of watering.

LIGHT

Among the many perennial flowers that successfully grow on the prairies the requirement for sunlight varies all the way from full sun for at least six hours per day to constant full shade. Most plants require a fair amount of sunlight to flower at their best but many of these can be very attractive or even more attractive in partial shade. Plant size, leaf size, leaf color, and the overall textural appearance of plants are modified by the amount of light the plant receives. So when we talk about shade-loving and sun-loving plants we are referring to the level of light at which a plant will achieve its aesthetic excellence.

FIGURE 27.

Papaver orientale (Oriental poppy)

PLANTING AND TRANSPLANTING

The best time for planting or transplanting most perennials is in the spring when the soil becomes workable and new growth is just beginning. However, for the very early flowering kinds which may even be in flower by the time the soil can be worked, it is best to wait until flowering is complete. A few plants transplant best in the summer or early fall, again sometime after flowering has occurred. These plants are in an inactive state at this time and will recover from transplant shock more readily than at any other time of year (for example, Oriental poppies, irises, and peonies). After transplanting they are able to re-establish before the onset of winter. For details on rejuvenating old plants by dividing and transplanting see Propagation by Separation and Division in Chapter 1 – Propagating Perennials.

When you transfer container-grown plants or seedlings to the garden, or transplant divided plants, plant them to the same depth that they were growing previously. If the soil bed has been properly prepared to a good tilth there should be no compaction around the root system and the new transplants should adapt to their new location quickly. Watering in the plants with a starter solution at the time of planting is recommended. Starter solution is a highly soluble fertilizer high in phosphorus (eg., 10-52-10, or 10-52-17) dissolved in water at the rate recommended on the label and applied to the soil around each new transplant. Mulching of newly planted or transplanted perennials is also highly recommended to maintain even moisture around the roots until the plant is well established

SPACING

Spacing will vary with each kind of plant and how dense you want the planting to appear. However, the mature height, spread and vigor of growth are the main factors to consider. Large plants such as bleeding heart (*Dicentra spectabilis*) and peonies (*Paeonia* spp.) can occupy up to a cubic metre (cubic yard) of space and so should be planted 90 to 100 cm (3 ft.) apart from one another. The vast majority of perennials have about half the spread of peonies and are planted about 45 cm (18 in.) on center. Mat forming plants or ground covers such as mother-of-thyme or goutweed can be planted at various spacings depending on how quickly you want them to develop into a solid mat. Most recommended plant spacings should be considered as guidelines only.

FIGURE 28.

Paeonia (peony).

Ed Toop

FIGURE 29

Iris sibirica 'Pansey Purple'.

Gail Rankin

Designing Beds or Borders

The term *hardy herbaceous perennials* includes a tremendous number of kinds of plants, and among that group a large percentage have attributes that make them aesthetically pleasing. Because of their diversity, there are several advantages to growing them in mixed groups rather than beds of one kind or as individual specimens.

With careful planning, a border can be developed to provide a long season of blooms. Not only a long season of color will result but also a constantly changing pattern of colors and textures as each type reaches its climax of beauty and fades away.

Brian Porter

FIGURE 30.

Dianthus plumarius (grass pinks) provide year-round interest and early summer blooms.

Plants are chosen not only for their color of bloom and season of flowering but also for their growth habit and mature height and in some cases for the color and texture of foliage. Because individual flowers are seldom pure in color but rather a combination of tints, shades, and tones of pure color or **hue,** or even a

FIGURE 31.

Chrysanthemums provide brilliant fall color.

FIGURE 32.

Traditional perennial border.

FIGURE 33.

Mixed border.

combination of hues, there are very few perennials that clash with one another. Another advantage of grouping is the opportunity to place plants with similar environmental requirements together. Even within a single moderately sized bed or border there are usually various microclimates involving shade, drainage, protection from wind, and other factors that can be used to advantage. In fact the spatial relationships of the various plants in an established border planting create their own microclimates.

Other aspects to keep in mind when choosing plant material are the extent of the flowering period and the color and texture of the flowers. Plant size and foliage color and texture are also important considerations. A series of contrasts of either color or form, or both, provide interest and rhythm from one end of a bed or border to the other. A well planned planting produces a harmony of changing colors, textures, and forms. There must also be a sense of scale which is in keeping with the surroundings. Not only must the overall dimensions of the planting be in scale with the lot or yard size but the size and coarseness of the individual plants must be in scale as well. A large flower border backed by a shrub border or woodlot on an acreage or farm could readily accommodate large-leafed, tall and bushy plants which would be totally out of place in a relatively small border on an average sized urban residential lot. There are four types of borders:

TRADITIONAL PERENNIAL BORDER

The traditional herbaceous perennial border is composed entirely of hardy herbaceous perennials. It may have a tree-shrub border, hedge, fence or wall as a backdrop, or it may be free-standing as in an "island bed". Such beds or borders are usually most effective if they are 3 to 5 m (9 to 15ft.) deep or wide and greater than 10 m (30 ft.) long. This limits their use as the dimensions suitable for a small residential lot could be as small as 1.5 m by 5 m (5 ft. by 15 ft.).

MIXED BORDER

The mixed border is perhaps the most popular for the home grounds since it incorporates shrubs and bedding plants with the herbaceous perennials to extend the season of bloom, and bedding plants are used to replace early spring bulbs after they die back. If a mixed border is well planned so that the woody plants do not compete unfavorably with the herbaceous ones, little maintenance is necessary.

RESERVE BORDER

If you have a fairly large perennial border you may want to maintain a reserve border. This is common in large public show gardens but can also be done for residential gardens as well. A small plot in the vegetable garden or orchard is set aside to maintain replacement specimens for plants which may die out in the show border. Autumn flowering chrysanthemums, for instance, may be grown from rooted cuttings in the spring in a reserve border, and transplanted to the show border in late summer. They could act as a replacement for earlier flowering bulbs.

CUT FLOWER BORDER

The cut flower border is a planting of perennials that are well adapted for cut flower use, plants with long stemmed blooms that are long lasting or produce flowers intermittently over a long period. Such a planting could be part of a reserve border as well. If you are interested in having a continual supply of cut flowers it is much more satisfactory to have a special garden plot for this purpose than to continually rob the show border.

CHOOSING A SITE

A site that receives full sun for six hours or more per day provides a suitable environment for the largest variety of perennials that bloom abundantly. However, many plants that bloom most abundantly in full sun will still flower in partial shade and may even be more attractive overall with reduced sunlight. In addition, a number of perennials require partial shade or even full shade in order to achieve

Alberta Horticultural Association

FIGURE 34.

Cut flower border.

their ultimate in attractiveness, be it flowers, foliage or overall shape. A given site may have a variety of **microclimates** with respect to hours of sunlight or shelter from wind and rain because of nearby hedges, shrubs, trees, buildings or fences. Once a flower bed has been developed the plants within it will also have an effect on the environment within the bed itself.

You may choose to develop an open flower bed (island bed) to be viewed from all sides rather than the conventional border along a property line backed by a fence, wall, hedge or other structure. The placement of plants in relation to height will, of course, vary depending upon the setting. An island bed will not have the same protection from wind as a border and is best limited to low and medium height plants with the taller plants placed in the middle of the bed. On the other hand, a large border planting with good wind protection can accommodate very tall plants [2 m (6 ft.) and over] at the back of the planting.

Hugh Knowles

FIGURE 35.

Large-leafed, coarse-textured plants need to be in scale with their surroundings.

FIGURE 36.

Aegopodium podograria 'Variegatum': some plants do well in sun and shade.

FIGURE 37.

Open bed viewed from all sides.

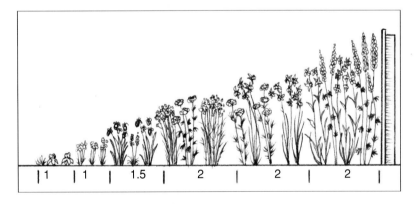

FIGURE 38.

Six height zones in proportions of 1:1:1.5:2:2:2.

CHOOSING A SHAPE

A bed or border may be rather formal with a geometric shape, such as a rectangle, or informal with a natural looking curved edge and variable width or depth. Avoid a patterned or scalloped edging, however, because it detracts from the beauty of the flowers. A natural edge that interfaces with the lawn, a turf walkway or possibly a paved walkway is preferable to a raised edging of stones or brick. The ultimate in tackiness is a row of painted stones. An edging of bricks or similar material laid flat and flush with the lawn is a compromise that is unobtrusive yet reduces the maintenance normally required with a direct lawn-border interface. A simple and effective way to develop a natural looking curvature to a bed or border edge is to lay down a piece of rope or flexible garden hose to outline the desired shape. Be sure that any curvature on the lawn-garden interface will accommodate easy access with the lawnmower. You can then spade the bed out to this traced marking.

PREPARING A PLAN

Once you have chosen the site, prepare a plan to scale on paper. The dimensions of the bed or border will vary depending on the site but the width should be in the range of 1.5 to 5 m (5 to 15 ft.). The overall size will depend upon the space available and the scale of the project. The dimensions must be in proportion with the size of the property be it a city lot, park, acreage, or farm.

HEIGHT

Once the bed or border has been outlined to scale on paper, you can arbitrarily designate height zones on the plan. Up to six basic height zones can be selected depending on the width of the overall bed or border as follows:

Edging material

- small, compact plants 15 to 25 cm (6 to 10 in.) in height.

Foreground material

- low perennials [30 to 45 cm (12 to 18 in.)], generally spring blooming including early spring flowering bulbs
- lance-leafed plants such as iris and daylilies.

Middleground material

- this section will accommodate the bulk of mid-summer flowering, medium height plants averaging about 75 cm (30 in.) but ranging in height from 50 to 85 cm (20 to 33 in.).

Background material

- tall flowering plants ranging in height from 90 to 120 cm (3 to 4 ft.)
- very tall plants ranging in height from 120 to 180 cm (4 to 6 ft.).

The suggested proportions for the width of the above six zones are 1:1:1.5:2:2:2. Making the zones at the rear of the border wider than those at the front takes into account perspective, thus giving the border the appearance of greater depth than it really has. For the average residential lot, a total of four height zones or less is probably more practical, especially if the width or depth is under 4 m (13 ft.).

COLOR

Planning what flower colors to include can be as sophisticated as you wish to make it. Fortunately very few flowers clash with one another, especially among natural species. In large measure this is because most flowers are a mixture of hues rather than pure individual colors. Therefore, a random mixture of plants

FIGURE 39.

Garden showing gradual height changes.

Gail Rankin

FIGURE 40.

Random color.

Alberta Horticultural Association

with respect to color can be very satisfying and attractive. However, to make the project more challenging you may wish to design a planting that is **monochromatic**, **complementary** or **analogous** in its color scheme.

The **Birren system** for outdoor color uses six basic colors which are listed here in descending order of the amount of light reflected from each (a value scale):

White 80%	Yellow 55%	Green 35%
Red 25%	Blue 20%	Black 0%

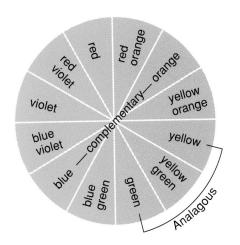

FIGURE 41.

FIGURE 42.

FIGURE 43.

Masses of high value color are not too effective in full sunlight; they tend to produce glare. For those borders located in strong sunlight, lower values should predominate. In shady borders, colors of high value can be used more freely. In deep shade, colors which possess a high degree of luminosity (orange and scarlet) are more satisfactory than yellow or white in spite of the fact that both yellow and white have higher color values.

Flower colors are seldom pure. Usually they are tints, shades or tones of the pure color or hue.

Tints are derived from yellow, green, red, or blue by the addition of white. Shades of these colors are obtained by the addition of black. Tones result from the addition of grey.

In each case (tint, shade or tone), as a measure of white, black or grey is added to a pure color, that color decreases in strength or purity. This decrease is said to be a decrease in **chroma**.

In spite of the fact that light, climate and humidity play an important part in the way colors can be arranged in the landscape, it is still possible to use either complementary (those opposite each other on the color wheel) or analogous colors (those which adjoin one another in the color wheel) for harmonious results.

Suggested Combinations
Blue
- With scarlet and buff.
- With white and yellow.
- With orange and scarlet.
- With yellow or orange of the same chroma (but use sparingly).

Violet, Purple and Magenta
(These colors lie between red and blue.)
- Those hues nearer blue: group together or use with tints and shades of blue.
- Those hues nearer red: group together or use with tints or shades of red.
- Violet or purple should be used with plenty of yellow or yellow-green foliage.
- Violet and purple can be contrasted with whites and yellows of equal chroma.

Red and Scarlet

- With dense green backgrounds.
- For sharp contrast, with white or clear blue.
- With analogous hues, red-violet and red-orange.

Pink (Tint of Red)

- Will gain more strength if interspersed with white.
- Goes well with other colors of the same chroma.

Orange

- With darker colors: red, browns and bronzes.
- With turquoise blue (complementary).
- With purple flowers and bright green foliage (split complementary).
- With creamy white or yellow.

Yellow

- With blue of equal chroma.
- With white (but use sparingly).
- Small amounts will liven up cold, heavy compositions.

White

- Frequently turns out to be a tint of one color or another. If so, use with other chromas of same color, or as a contrast with that color's complement.
- If interspersed among low value colors, it softens them.
- If interspersed among high value colors, it strengthens them.

Greens

There are a great many foliage greens varying from deep, dull green through to the darkest of the evergreens. Foliage color must be secondary to flower colors and be carefully chosen to intensify the effect of anything placed in front of it. Thus, yellow-green or blue-green foliage can spoil the effect of a carefully arranged harmony that does not go well with yellow or blue.

Grey and Silvery Foliage

Grey and silvery foliage can be used to lighten heavy or monotonous masses of dark green and, at the same time, heighten the effect of distance.

FIGURE 44.

Red/scarlet/dark green combination.

FIGURE 45.

Complementary colors

FIGURE 46.

Silver/grey in a planting.

FIGURE 47a.

Aconitum napellus 'Bicolor'

FIGURE 47b.

Gaillardia x *aristata*

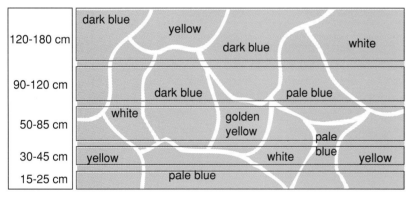

120-180 cm	dark blue, yellow, dark blue, white	
90-120 cm	dark blue, pale blue	
50-85 cm	white, golden yellow, pale	
30-45 cm	yellow, white, blue, yellow	
15-25 cm	pale blue	

FIGURE 48.

Planning a perennial bed based on height and color zones.

They can also bring conflicting colors into pleasing relationships. They are ineffective when dotted among bright colors, but effective in similar surrounding if used in mass. Grey and silvery foliage is most effective with light-tinted flowers.

Flower colors are seldom pure; in addition, the colors present are usually tints, shades, or tones of pure hues (Figure 47a and b). Light tints are often referred to as pastels. One of the ways to intensify the hue of pastel flowers is to plant white flowers next to them. Similarly plants with grey or silvery foliage are most effective when planted next to light-tinted flowers. An excellent way to use white flowered and/or silvery-grey foliaged plants is in a "white" or "night" garden. A night garden makes extensive use of white, pink, and light yellow flowering perennials as well as those which are fragrant. It also employs perennials with grey foliage. Such an area might also include a small tree with white or pink blossoms (eg. 'Thunderchild' crabapple) whose trunk and canopy could be illuminated with subtle lighting from a hidden source. Include a classic bench for two under the tree and the night garden is complete.

Once you have decided on the color scheme, draw a color distribution plan, perhaps as an overlay for the basic plan which contains the height zones. Individual color zones will overlap two or possibly more height zones across the entire layout for the bed or border. As a further aid to planning, you may wish to combine the height-color distribution plan with one that considers the seasonal distribution of flowers. Figure 49a identifies the placement of perennials that bloom in fall. The placement of summer flowering perennials is identified in Figure 49b and the placement of spring flowering perennials is identified in Figure 49c. The method for designing a seasonal distribution plan for a perennial border is detailed below.

PERENNIALS FOR THE PLAINS AND PRAIRIES

PUTTING THE PLAN ON PAPER

To make sure of an attractive combination of flowers blooming in a perennial border through spring, summer and fall, sketch the locations of plants on sheets of tracing paper laid over an outline of the bed. If you use the height-color distribution plan as the bed outline (Figure 48), your final plan will include height-color distribution as well. On the first sheet of tracing paper, select tall fall-blooming varieties; draw these in as clumps (light green) spaced along the back. Then add complementary fall plants (also indicated in light green), placing medium-sized ones in the center and short ones towards the front (see Figure 49a).

On a second sheet of tracing paper laid over the first, plan your summer blooms. Since most plants that flower in summer are medium-sized, select these first as your main display; draw these in as clumps, concentrating them in the center of the bed and locating the plants (indicated in medium green) in some of the open areas not already occupied by fall flowers. Then place in front and back a few tall and short summer-blooming varieties whose colors will complement the flower you have chosen for the center.

On a third sheet of tracing paper laid over the other two, plan your spring-blooming plants (dark green) in the remaining spaces (see Figure 49c). As most spring perennials are short, they naturally look best in the front of the bed. Some medium-sized and tall spring-flowering plants should be interspersed in the center and back. Now you can trace the outlines of your fall and summer displays through to the top sheet. If your seasonal distribution plan was created in conjunction with the height-color distribution plan, you are ready to select and determine perennial border plants that reflect height, color, and season of bloom considerations.

Any gaps on the finalized plan can be filled with bulbs or annuals. Although height must be taken into consideration to prevent taller plants from hiding shorter ones, there

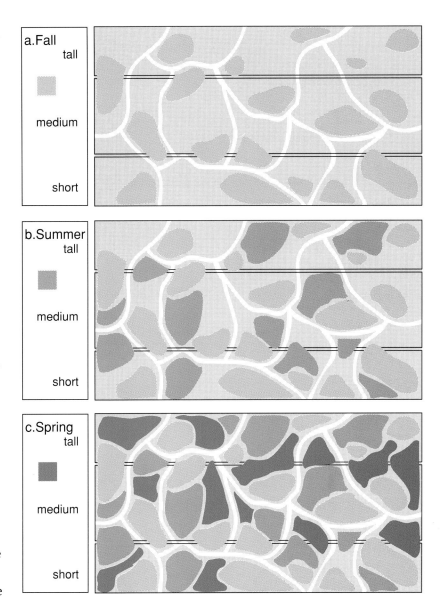

should not be a rigid demarcation of height. A gentle blending of the planned height zones prevents monotony. Once this has been achieved, choose specific plants (using the reference charts in this book with nursery catalogs) for each designated height-color area and seasonal distribution area. For convenience at planting time, include a legend in the margin of the plan that details the mature spread of the plant and the time and length of its blooming period.

To achieve succession of bloom, considerable planning is required for perennial flower beds and borders.

FIGURE 49.

Planning a perennial border for seasonal distribution of flowers.

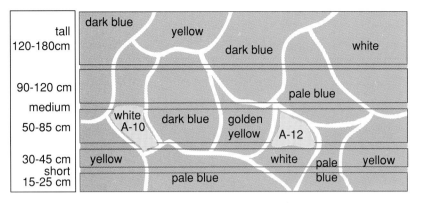

tall 120-180cm	dark blue yellow dark blue	white
90-120 cm medium 50-85 cm	pale blue white A-10 dark blue golden yellow A-12	
30-45 cm short 15-25 cm	yellow white pale yellow pale blue blue	

FIGURE 50.

Selecting plants.

In summary, the four steps to follow in planning a perennial border are:

1. Create a scale drawing of the planned bed.
2. Select the number of height zones and define these on the plan.
3. Select the color combinations desired and place them on the plan.
4. Select specimens on the basis of height, color, and season of bloom.

You are now ready to choose plants that fit the criteria for height and color specified on the plan.

FIGURE 51.

Preparation of beds.

SELECTING PLANTS

Assemble a planting list for the plants chosen for the border giving the height, season of bloom, color and total number of plants required. If you assign a code letter to each kind of plant listed, those letters can be placed on the plan to designate the exact locations. A number can follow the letter to indicate how many plants are required at each location, for example, A-3, A-10, B-1, etc. (see Figure 50). For groupings of less than 10 plants, an odd number rather than an even number is generally more effective. Large, bulky plants such as peonies can be very effective as individual specimens. Unlike bedding plants, most perennials are more effective in small groupings than in mass plantings. However, the repetition of groups of a particular kind across the border is important to provide a sense of balance and unity to the planting. Greater interest can also be achieved by shifting some of the groups out of their height zones as designated on the plan. Some contrast in height, form and possibly even blooming season can be achieved by moving some plants or groups of plants either forward or backward from their position on the basic plan.

EXECUTING THE PLAN

There are three aspeccts to executing the plan. The first is preparing the site, next comes the actual planting, and last is making adjustments.

SITE PREPARATION

Begin by measuring and staking out the site. Next, remove or transplant sod and other plant materials from the site. The bed is now ready for soil preparation prior to planting. Since the plants to be used are perennial, prepare the soil thoroughly to ensure strong permanent root development and a minimum of maintenance weed control. If the site is weedy, you may want to treat it with a herbicide such as glyphosate (available under various trade names) or keep the site fallow for one growing season, or both.

It is also important that the soil be in good tilth to a reasonable depth to ensure good drainage and unrestricted root development. To ensure this, systematically deep spade the entire

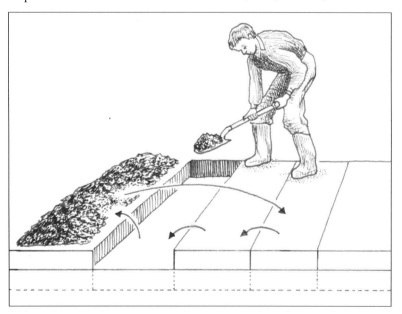

bed or border. Start at one end of the bed and remove one spade width of the top 15 cm (6 in.) of soil the full width of the border and stockpile this for use later (Figures 51 and 52a). Then use a deep spade to turn the remaining subsoil an additional 20 or 30 cm (8 to 12 in.) down (Figure 52c). This is often referred to as "double-digging". It is possible to substitute a rototiller for the spade to do the actual digging, but a combination of spading and rototilling does the best job. Compost, well rotted manure or peat can be incorporated with this subsoil to increase the organic matter content and improve the soil structure. Fertilizer could also be incorporated, particularly one high in phosphorus such as superphosphate (0-20-0), treble or triple phosphate (0-45-0) or ammonium phosphate (11-48-0) (Figure 52b). Treble phosphate and ammonium phosphate should be applied at a rate of approximately 1 kg/10m^2 (2 lb./100 ft.^{2}). A soil test of both the top soil (at 15 cm or 6 in. depth) and the subsoil (at 30 cm or 12 in. depth) will indicate what nutrients are in low supply and what type of fertilizer will correct the deficiencies. Since most prairie soils tend to be low in phosphorus, the incorporation of a fertilizer containing phosphorus is a good general recommendation if a soil test is not conducted.

Once this first strip of subsoil has been turned and any additives incorporated, the top soil [15 cm (6 in.)] in the adjoining strip can be spaded over onto the strip of modified subsoil and the whole process repeated across the length of the entire bed. The final step is to move the stockpiled soil from the original digging and place it on the last strip of modified subsoil. Allow the deeply tilled bed to settle several weeks or perhaps over winter before you plant. Incorporate fertilizer and peat or compost into the top soil of the entire bed after the deep spading is complete, either by spade or rototiller, and shortly before planting. Again, fertilizer application based on soil test results is best, but in lieu of a soil analysis a fertilizer such as 10-30-10 applied at a rate of 700 g to 1 kg per 10 m^2 (1.5 to 2 lb./100 ft^2) is recommended.

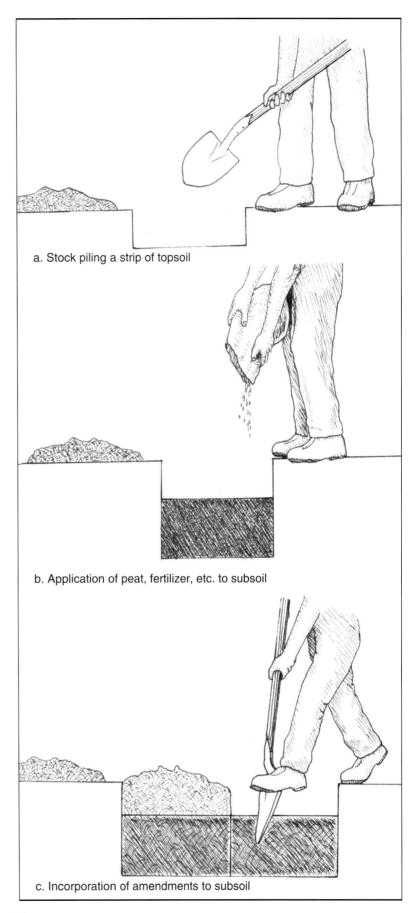

a. Stock piling a strip of topsoil

b. Application of peat, fertilizer, etc. to subsoil

c. Incorporation of amendments to subsoil

FIGURE 52. Double digging.

PLANTING

Young plants, either seedlings or rooted cuttings, or divisions from old plants may be planted out when the soil is settled and conditions are favorable. Most perennials are best planted in the spring but fall planting is best, or even mandatory, for certain kinds such as spring flowering bulbs, peonies, and most lilies. A good planting plan will aid greatly in ensuring proper placement and spacing. All transplants and bulbs should be well firmed and then watered in to ensure good soil contact with the roots or bulbs. Watering-in with a starter solution (e.g., 10-52-10 or 10-52-17 at dilution recommended on label) is recommended for transplants since it encourages rapid establishment of the roots.

Some discrepancies in numbers of plants required will likely occur between the plan and the actual placement of plants. Often fewer plants are required than the plan specifies unless you have had experience in this exercise.

ADJUSTING THE PLAN

After the border is finished and flourishing you may wish to make some changes. Mark with stakes or flags any plants which require removal or transplanting and make the changes when time permits or at a time best suited for transplanting. You may want to make changes to alleviate crowding, improve the overall distribution of blooms, or separate color combinations that do not blend well. Keep in mind that growth patterns, time of blooming and sequence of blooming vary somewhat from one season to the next. It is this variability in part which makes gardening such an interesting enterprise. Furthermore, the different kinds of plants vary in vigor and rate of growth. Some will require division or replacement every three or four years whereas others may remain undisturbed for ten years or more.

Routine

Care

Routine care consists of vigilant weeding and cultivating, timely watering, regular fertilizing and mulching, periodic renovating, constant insect and disease control, and spring or fall cleanup and preparation for winter.

WEEDING AND CULTIVATING

Once perennial flowers have been planted, eternal vigilance for the appearance of weeds is very important. If you allow unwanted plants to become established in and among the crowns of the perennial flowers it is very difficult to eradicate them. The establishment of perennial weed species can be particularly troublesome since they can compete with the flowers on the same terms. They are usually more vigorous and aggressive and hence flourish to the detriment of the flowers. Annual weeds, on the other hand, must start each new growing season as seedlings and are thus easier to control than established more mature plants. Most effective herbicides will generally remove the ornamental plants as well as the weeds. Pre-emergence herbicides that will kill germinating seeds without destroying the buds in plant crowns are really the only practical chemical controls. However, these are not usually available to the home gardener, nor are they recommended.

Regular shallow cultivation is the best weed control approach for the non-commercial gardener. It destroys young weeds and weed seedlings before they can become fully established. Cultivation also prevents surface crusting of the soil thereby maintaining good aeration and rapid percolation of rain or irrigation water into the soil. Spading the soil and turning it over between the plants during fall cleanup destroys

FIGURE 53.

Hoeing between plants.

any weeds that may have established a "foot hold" in these spaces and helps to confine the spread of crowns of the more vigorous flowers. If the spaded surface is left "rough" it allows frost to act on the clumps of soil, thus improving soil structure and preventing soil compaction. A well planned and properly mulched bed with proper plant spacing will prevent weed seedlings from competing once a full canopy of foliage has developed to cover the ground.

WATERING

Proper watering is the key to successful gardening. Although you have little control over natural precipitation, you can ensure a well structured soil with good drainage properties to reduce the potentially devastating effects of too much water. In addition, you have control of irrigation water to supplement natural precipitation to allow healthy plants to achieve their full potential.

WATER HOLDING CAPACITY OF SOIL

The water holding capacity of a soil can be adjusted or modified through the addition of

peat, compost, sand or even clay. The higher the clay content of a soil the higher its water holding capacity. Organic matter such as peat or compost also has a high water holding capability. It is interesting that a clay soil high in organic matter will not only hold more water than a clay soil lacking organic matter but it will have better drainage properties. Organic matter causes the fine clay particles to aggregate into a crumb-like structure creating pore spaces. However, when mixed with sand, organic matter has a binding effect. In short, the addition of organic matter to any type of soil is beneficial.

Much of the water requirements of plants can be met through soil modification. For example, plants with a high water requirement or requiring a constantly moist situation will do best in soils high in organic matter, particularly a clay loam, whereas plants that thrive under hot dry conditions will do best in sandy soils with low to moderate organic content. The chart below shows the water-holding capacity of the different soil textures.

Soil Texture	Water-Holding Capacity, %*
Sandy Loam	12 – 18
Silt Loam	24 – 32
Clay Loam	32 – 48
Peat	100+

* As a percentage of the dry soil weight.

HOW MUCH WATER?

Add sufficient water to permit percolation to a depth of 30 cm (1 ft.) or more. Deep watering encourages strong deep rooting but the actual depth needed depends upon the potential for rooting depth of the plants being watered. Some perennial flowers are capable of sending roots down 1 m (3 ft.) or more whereas others will form a mat of roots only 15 cm (6 in.) or less in depth regardless of the depth of moist soil. However, if moisture is not available beyond a certain depth, roots will not grow beyond that depth. (see Chapter 2, Figure 26). Even plants with the potential for deep rooting will only produce roots in the moist surface layer of soil if a dry zone separates this surface layer from moist subsoil. How and when you water depends upon weather conditions and the rate of water use by the plants.

FERTILIZING AND MULCHING

Regular incorporation of compost or well rotted manure will usually maintain an adequate balance of nutrients for perennials but many will perform better if given supplementary applications of a complete chemical fertilizer. An annual application of 10-30-10 or equivalent analysis ratio at 40 g to 50 g per m^2 (1 lb. per 100 ft.^{2}) is often suggested. If peat is used in place of compost or manure supplementary fertilization is definitely required. The use of water soluble fertilizer, such as 20-20-20, at the dilution rate recommended on the package and applied with a watering can is also an option. If particular plants in the border are showing "hunger" signs, use this method of applying supplemental fertilizer.

Organic mulch in the form of peat, uncontaminated grass clippings, wood chips, chopped straw, or other available material is very beneficial. It keeps the soil cool for plants that require a cool root zone. It helps to conserve soil moisture by preventing evaporation from the soil surface. It also replaces the need for cultivation to prevent crusting of the soil surface as well as encouraging micro-organism activity which in turn improves soil structure and the availability of nutrients to the plant roots. A mulch applied after freeze-up in the fall protects bulbs or the roots and crowns of other perennials from severe winter temperatures and the stress of alternate freezing and thawing.

RENOVATING OLD PLANTINGS

Vigorous plants such as chrysanthemums and woolly yarrow that spread rapidly usually require replanting every two or three years. As the plant expands, the center of the crown often

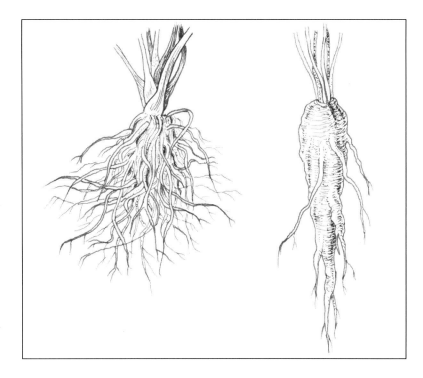

FIGURE 54.

Well-established root systems.

dies out. Replant a portion of the plant that shows good vigor. Incorporate compost or peat and some fertilizer high in phosphorus with the soil prior to replanting to aid in the plant's re-establishment.

Some plants such as columbine and Iceland poppy are short-lived perennials and may need replacement every three or four years. Quite often these kinds of plants self propagate by seed or natural layerage (or other forms of vegetative propagation). Remove the old dead plants and transplant some of the

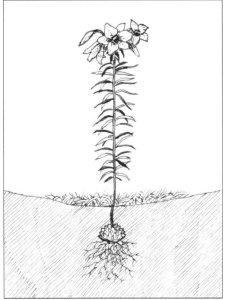

FIGURE 55.

Mulch.

COMPOSTING

Composting is a method used to decay plant and animal refuse by microbial action to form humus, a vital soil ingredient.

CONSTRUCTION OF A COMPOST PILE

Construction depends on your preference, and situation. No structure at all offers complete flexibility in the movement of the pile. Unprotected compost piles must be kept moist at all times by frequent waterings. A structure can be provided by using grass sods as walls, building a bottomless wooden box of convenient dimensions with a lid, or digging a pit for which a cover or lid is provided.

The conventional system for composting is to place the organic wastes in layers approximately 15 cm (6 in.) thick, alternating with layers of old grass sods or soil. The material is watered down and kept moist at all times. It should be forked occasionally to avoid overheating, but is generally kept covered and relatively undisturbed for one to two years, until it is thoroughly decayed.

A newer method developed at the University of California, Berkeley, provides for high temperature and rapid composting through improved aeration. While it requires considerable labor, its advantages lie in the absence of foul odors and a rapid recycling of wastes. It is this method that is well adapted to the urban scene.

THE FRAME

A wooden frame with either slatted or wire mesh side walls and a capacity of about 1 m³ (about 1 yd.³) is adequate for the average residential lot. It should have no top or bottom and will, therefore, require sturdy construction to retain its shape. It should be lightweight with the sides slightly tapered toward the top for easy removal when the pile requires turning. To turn the pile, lift off the frame, set it beside the pile, and fork the compost back into the empty frame. A single-bin or two-bin frame can also be used with posts set into the ground.

With this type of construction, a removable front panel is required.

PROCEDURE

Autumn is a good time to start a compost pile since there is an abundance of materials available at that time. Store all garden cleanup materials in the compost box until spring. Larger material should be cut up into 20 to 25 cm (8 to 10 in.) lengths for better consolidation and easier future handling. Little, if any, decomposition will occur over the cold winter months. In the spring, add rakings and the first grass clippings, turning the pile to mix the old and new material. Add water if the material is dry. The pile will usually heat up within three days. Continue to add grass clippings and other materials as they become available and turn the pile at least once a week. Frequent turning and thorough mixing is essential to supply air to the interior of the pile. Add water as the pile is turned to provide uniform moisture throughout the pile. Enough moisture is present when the particles of compost glisten. Foul odors indicate too much moisture; the remedy is more frequent turning to speed up evaporation and improve aeration. Once the odors disappear, resume the regular routine of turning every five to seven days.

At the end of August, stop adding additional material but continue to turn the pile and keep it moist. Fall cleanup material can be used to start a new pile for composting the following season. It is finished when the pile will not heat up even though moisture and air are adequate. Finished compost is a uniformly dark color with an earthy odor. Shredding it with a mechanical shredder makes it easier to incorporate into the garden soil.

THE COMPOSTING PROCESS

Composting is brought about by the activity of bacteria, fungi, and actinomycetes. All these organisms are present in garden residues. No additives, such as compost starter, fertilizer, lime or soil are necessary to make the pile work. The first organisms involved in this process are active at ambient temperatures. These are succeeded by organisms active at successively higher temperatures. The internal temperature of a small compost pile of the type described here will reach 55 to 65°C (130 to 150°F) or more. This range of temperature is high enough to kill flies (in all stages of development), weed seeds, and plant disease organisms.

Composting organisms require a suitable carbon:nitrogen ratio for peak activity. Mixing dry garden wastes (high carbon:nitrogen ratio) with grass clippings (low carbon:nitrogen ratio) usually produces a suitable ratio. If the ratio is too high, sprinkle in nitrogen fertilizer (such as 21-0-0 or 33-0-0) on each successive layer of the pile to improve the balance.

FIGURE 56.

Composting

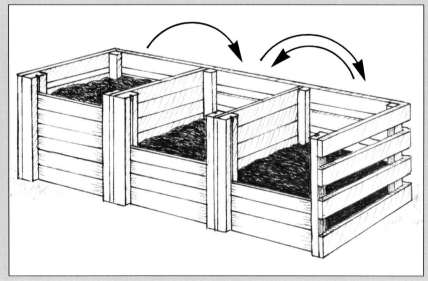

vigorous seedlings or shoots on a regular basis to maintain an ordered planting.

Whenever an existing perennial flower border requires any major renovation, it provides the opportunity for redesigning the entire planting. All the plants can be lifted, divided and/or separated as required and the soil improved through the incorporation of organic matter, fertilizer and deep cultivation. Always select the most vigorous specimens for replanting.

INSECT AND DISEASE CONTROL

You can do much to control disease and plant pests without resorting to chemical pesticides. One of the advantages of growing perennials in a prairie climate is the almost complete absence of major insect or disease problems. The first line of attack is to start with healthy plant material and provide the proper care to keep it healthy and vigorous. The second line of attack is to take action quickly when you discover pests or disease. The third line of attack is sanitation. This is particularly important in the control of botrytis which can be a problem on lilies and to a lesser extent on peonies and irises. Remove dead flowers and leaves as soon as possible during the growing season and remove all top growth before the onset of winter or alternatively in early spring before new growth starts. If this clean up is delayed until spring you run the risk of infection from overwintered pathogens or an outbreak of other pests that have survived in the debris.

Another good practice in preventing the spread of such diseases as botrytis is to avoid wetting the foliage when watering the plants. Some diseases, such as mildew, are often controlled by planting resistant cultivars (eg. such as 'Marshall's Delight' monarda).

Despite good management and proper care pest problems and disease will arise on occasion. When they do, take immediate action

FIGURE 57.

Fall clean-up.

to have the pest or disease identified and apply the appropriate controls. (See *Insect Pests of the Prairies*, a companion book of this series and the *University of Alberta Home Gardening Course* section dealing with plant diseases.)

FALL CLEAN-UP AND PREPARATION FOR WINTER

Remove all dead and dying top growth in perennial flower beds before the onset of winter to prevent the overwintering of possible pathogens or insects in the debris. Although this debris can act as a mulch and snowtrap over winter, it is safer to add a clean mulch or peat, or provide a snow fence or other wind breaking device to trap snow. Spading or turning over the soil between the plant crowns also helps trap snow.

There are several things you can do to help bring plants through the harsh winter. A good snow cover that remains in place throughout the winter season is ideal. You may need to periodically shovel or transport snow from one part of the garden to another. The orientation of flower beds in relation to buildings, fences, trees, and shrubs (especially coniferous evergreens) will determine how much snow accumulates and also how long it remains unmelted. If you have to contend with chinook conditions of alternate freezing and thawing throughout the winter, this presents a real challenge. The use of a thick layer of organic mulch is often recommended when good snow cover is not a viable option. However, this can lead to disaster. The rapid melting of snow followed by the sudden return of freezing temperatures will saturate such mulches and turn them into virtually solid masses of ice. This destroys the insulating properties of the mulch and greatly reduces the oxygen supply to the living crowns and roots of the plants underneath. It also provides an ideal environment for snow mold to develop. Although snow mold is a disease of turf grass, it can also affect other ground covers in the vicinity of diseased turf. The only alternatives are to not mulch at all, or to provide a snow absorbent or water shedding cover of some sort. This may be feasible for individual plants and is, for example, recommended for tea roses, but is rather a major project for an entire perennial border.

Hardy Bulbs:

A Showy

Parade

Spring flowering bulbs are not a particularly popular group of perennials in the prairie region for a variety of reasons. They are sometimes not available from suppliers until late in the fall when soil is partially frozen. They require fall planting with a few weeks of warm, moist soil conditions before freeze-up in order to establish a root system. If this doesn't happen, the bulbs may not even emerge from the soil the following spring, let alone produce any flowers.

Another reason they are often shunned is because their flowering can be very erratic, depending on the microclimate around each bulb. A third reason is that many of the bulbs offered for sale are not hardy enough to survive the prairie climate. In late winter and early spring, the soil within our gardens thaws and warms up at variable rates depending on the amount of exposure to the sun's penetrating rays or the distance away from the foundations of the buildings, especially heated ones. Bulbs of a given kind, for example, daffodils, may flower any time between late March and early July depending on where they are planted. If they flower very early, they may get cut down by a killing frost before they reach maturity.

Although these negative comments are given as a caution to the novice, hardy spring bulbs should still be tried. There are a number of kinds, including species and cultivars of *Narcissus, Tulipa, Crocus, Scilla* and related **genera** that can be a delight in the prairie garden if given the right niche.

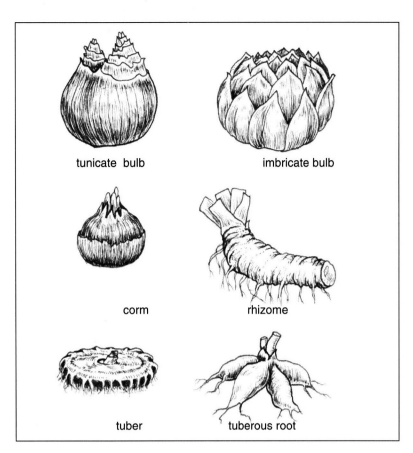

FIGURE 58. Types of bulbs and related structures.

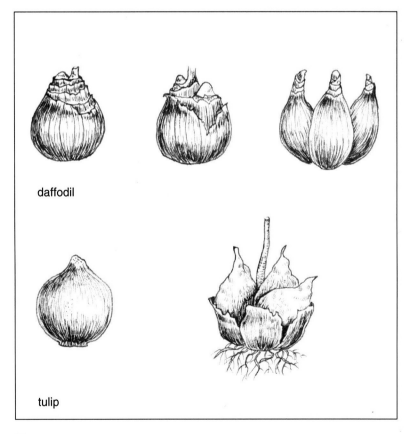

FIGURE 59. Daffodil and tulip division.

A number of perennial plants produce some sort of underground storage organ which may be loosely referred to as a bulb. However, these plant organs vary in structure and many are actually **corms, tubers**, **rhizomes**, or **tuberous** roots rather than true bulbs. True bulbs are similar to large buds and are composed of a basal plate of rather hard tissue to which fleshy food-filled leaf bases are attached that may be tightly packed together, such as is the case with daffodils, or rather loosely arranged, such as lily bulbs (see Figure 58 for a diagram of the tunicate bulb and imbricate bulb). Corms, tubers, and rhizomes, on the other hand, are made up of rather hard stem tissue filled with stored food. Most of our hardy bulbous plants tend to have true bulbs or rhizomes, whereas the non-hardy tend to be corms or tubers.

True bulbs in themselves vary somewhat in structure and in their method of propagation. Daffodils and tulips both have tunicate bulbs, (see Figure 59) yet multiply at much different rates. When they are purchased for planting in the fall, they are in a resting or "dormant" state and the roots are not present. The flowers, however, are present inside the bulb, perfectly formed, in a very minute state (see Figure 60). To bloom properly, they require the development of roots followed by a cold period (winter) of several months.

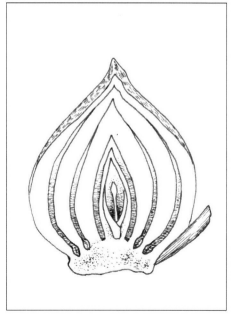

FIGURE 60. Cut away tulip bulb.(tunicate type).

Those plants able to survive our winter season without the bulbs being lifted and stored indoors over winter and planted out in the spring are "hardy". Bulbs that have proved hardy across the prairie region include species of *Tulipa, Muscari, Scilla, Puschkinia, Fritillaria, Ixiolirion, Allium,* and *Lilium. Hyacinthus, Narcissus,* and *Crocus* are generally not hardy in the colder regions, but will survive in the milder regions of the area, particularly in sheltered locations. Plants such as *Dahlias, Gladiolus,* or *Canna* can successfully grow and flower in our gardens, but their storage organs will not live through the winter if left in the ground. These plants must be handled like bedding plants and are treated more like annual flowers than perennials.

USES IN THE LANDSCAPE

Hardy bulbs can be incorporated successfully into herbaceous perennial borders. Summer flowering lilies and alliums pose no special problems. However, early flowering bulbs are unattractive after flowering, yet must be left to die back naturally if they are to survive and flower again the following spring. To screen the dying foliage, plant them with ground covers, such as moss phlox or woolly thyme, or **interplant** them with bedding plants after the blooms fade. In public show gardens, spring flowering bulbs are usually lifted after flowering and heeled into a reserve area of the nursery for maturation of the foliage and regeneration of the bulbs (Figure 62). After total **senescence**, they are dug, cleaned, and stored in preparation for replanting at summer's end.

Ribbon plantings along sidewalks are an attractive way to use bulbs to provide an early spring display of color. They can be followed later by bedding plants.

A third way to utilize bulbs is to plant small groupings of them as accents in front of evergreen shrubs in shrub borders or **foundation plantings**. A great deal of "mileage" can be achieved from only a few bulbs when used in this manner.

Some kinds of bulbs, particularly daffodils, crocuses, and lilies, lend themselves

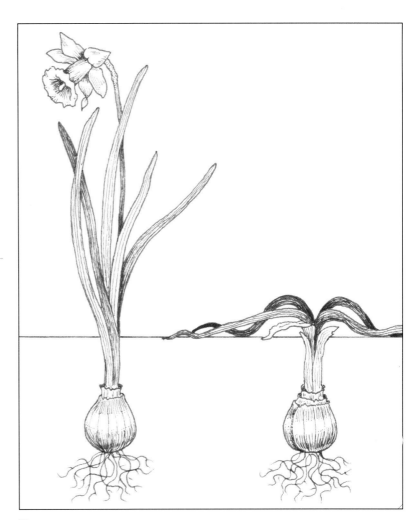

FIGURE 61. Natural dieback of *Narcissus* after flowering.

FIGURE 62. Heeling in spent bulbs to encourage maturation of foliage.

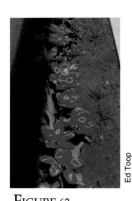

FIGURE 63.

Ribbon planting.

to naturalized plantings in turf or at the edges of wooded areas or shrub borders. To achieve a naturalized appearance to a planting, place the bulbs in a pail and toss them gently onto the ground with a sweeping motion of the pail. Plant them where they fall, removing some that are too thick. The distance between bulbs should be around 12 to 20 cm (5 to 8 in.), depending on the kind of bulbs and the ultimate size of the plants. Some irregularity in spacing is desirable even in normal bed or border plantings.

Many of the short dainty spring bulbs lend themselves to planting in rock gardens. These even include dwarf species of narcissus and tulips such as *Tulipa tarda*.

Keep in mind the height of the flowers when you select a location. Small flowers will appear lost in a distant border. Shorter bulbs with dainty blooms are best planted near a walkway, entrance, or patio where they can be seen and appreciated at close range.

PREPARATION FOR PLANTING

SOIL PREPARATION

Dig the soil to a depth of at least 20 to 25 cm (8 to 10 in.) and incorporate about 5 cm (2 in.) of peat moss, compost, or well-rotted manure. For lilies, prepare the soil to a depth of 45 cm (18 in.), particularly for the stem-rooting types. To achieve good soil depth and good drainage, lilies are often grown in raised beds. The incorporation of fertilizer, especially one containing phosphorus is also recommended. Bone meal, 11-52-0, and 10-30-10, are usually good choices. Recommended rates of application are 50 to 150 g/m^2 (1.5 to 5 oz. /10ft.^{2}) for bone meal, and 50 g/m^2 (1 lb./100 ft.^{2}) for 11-52-0 or 10-30-10. Have the soil tested to determine exactly what fertilizer should be used and at what rate.

PURCHASING

Purchase good quality bulbs from a reputable dealer or catalogue. Generally, the larger the bulb, the better the flowers, although size will vary from species to species and even between cultivars of a given species. Look for the following characteristics that are indicative of good quality:

- Plumpness and firmness. There should be no feeling of squishiness or looseness when the bulb is compressed in the hand.
- Weight. It should feel as if it has good solid mass or substance to it.
- Clean skin or surface free from blemishes. Carelessly handled bulbs show corky spots or even fungus growth on the scales.

TIMING

Spring flowering and even summer flowering bulbs such as lilies and flowering onions (*Alliums*) are planted in the fall. They should be planted as soon as they are available in late summer or early fall. They must be planted early enough to allow the establishment of a good root system before the ground freezes, preferably a **minimum of 10 days**.

DEPTH

The depth of planting varies with the kind and size of bulb, but **deeper planting is suggested for the prairie region**. Since lily bulbs have live roots attached to the bulbs, these roots must be evenly spread out and soil worked in and around them so that no air pockets develop. (See Figure 64 for suggested planting depths.)

Depth of planting is a function of soil type as well as size and species of bulb. Bulbs should be planted 3 to 5 cm (1 to 2 in.) deeper in sandy soils than in heavy clay soils. Regardless of the soil type, good drainage is essential. Some lilies produce roots both from the base of the bulb and from the buried portion of the stem above the bulb. Such lilies are referred to as stem rooting lilies, as opposed to the regular or so-called basal rooting types. To maximize the potential for root formation, plant stem rooting lilies a little deeper than basal rooting lilies. Most of the hardy cultivars are stem rooting types. A notable exception is the native wood lily (*Lilium philadelphicum* var. andinum).

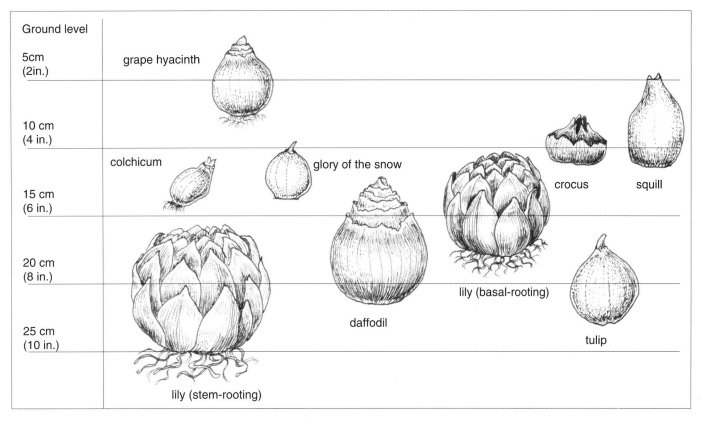

Ground level	
5cm (2in.)	grape hyacinth
10 cm (4 in.)	crocus squill
15 cm (6 in.)	colchicum glory of the snow
20 cm (8 in.)	lily (basal-rooting)
25 cm (10 in.)	daffodil tulip
	lily (stem-rooting)

FIGURE 64. Planting depth for bulbs.

CARE AND MAINTENANCE

If bulbs have been mulched with up to 5 cm (2 in.) of peat or grass clippings, you must remove the mulch early in the spring before the plants emerge. Mulches serve a double purpose. If applied right after planting, they delay the freezing of the ground, thus allowing more time for the bulbs to establish roots before winter. During the winter, mulches protect the bulbs from severe cold (see Figure 66).

If the mulch is not too deep it may not require removal in the spring. Once bulbs have emerged, a light cultivation between the plants will kill any germinating weed seeds and make it easier for rainwater to penetrate the soil. If a mulch is present no cultivation should be necessary. During the pre-flowering growing period, tulips in particular are very sensitive to drying. If the soil moisture content becomes low, the buds are almost certain to "**blast**" and fail to open. Therefore, for tulips at least, a moist soil during this period is critical and irrigations are usually necessary.

To encourage foliage development when plants are young, apply a light application of fertilizer high in nitrogen, such as ammonium

FIGURE 65. Stem rooting and basal rooting lily bulbs.

sulfate (21-0-0) at 30 to 50 g/m² (0.5 to 1 lb./100 ft.²). This ensures strong bulbs for future flowering. An application of a complete fertilizer after flowering is recommended for many kinds of bulbs [ie. 10-30-10 at 50 g/m² (1 lb./100 ft.²)]. To ensure the maintenance of strong bulbs from year to year, keep plants well watered and healthy until foliage begins to die back naturally . Remove fading flowers to prevent seed formation and encourage the development of strong bulbs. Old faded flowers present an untidy appearance and run the risk of becoming infected with pathogens such as **botrytis**. Bulbs that have been left undisturbed in the garden throughout the summer after their growth cycle is complete require moisture in the fall in order to develop strong new root systems for the new cycle of growth. Be sure to provide adequate moisture to all bulb plantings.

FIGURE 66.

Mulching bulbs for the winter season.

You can lift and replant bulbs any time after the foliage dies sufficiently to fall over. Bulbs can be replanted immediately, or air dried and stored in a warm, well-ventilated place until fall. There are three reasons for lifting and replanting hardy bulbs:
- To increase the number of flowering size bulbs of a given cultivar more rapidly.
- To rearrange a planting.
- To rejuvenate a planting that has become too crowded and has fallen off in flower size and number.

KINDS OF BULBS

TULIPS

Although we associate garden tulips with Holland, their country of origin is actually Turkey, with some 50 or so wild species of the genus *Tulipa* found scattered around the Mediterranean region and into Asia. Turkish gardeners made the best collections and bred and selected superior varieties. The Austrian ambassador to Turkey took bulbs to Vienna in the mid-1500s and by the end of that century they had been introduced into much of Europe, including Britain and Holland. Tulips became the rage in Holland by the 1630s with certain rare bulbs selling for several thousands of dollars apiece. Most of the garden types or cultivars often referred to as "Dutch" tulips are believed to be derived mainly from the species *Tulipa gesnerana*. Because of the tremendous range of variability among tulips, they have been classified into a number of divisions based on flower form, bloom time, and parentage (see Table 1).

In the early 1960s the Netherlands Flower Bulb Institute organized several tulip trials throughout the U.S. and Canada in order to obtain data on the adaptability of Dutch tulips to the various climate zones of North America. These trials were also instrumental in promoting the products of Dutch bulb growers to the new world markets. The University of Alberta at Edmonton, Canada, was the most northerly co-operator in this project. Bulbs of some 155 cultivars and species (mostly cultivars) were supplied for fall planting over a period of years (three separate plantings). Treatments consisted of two depths of planting with the three plantings serving essentially as replicates. Plantings were left undisturbed for a minimum of three seasons each.

Differences in response did occur among treatments and among cultivars and species, but they also occurred between plantings. Because of the variability of our climate and the unpredictability of our winter conditions in particular, no striking conclusions could be drawn. In general, all the cultivars performed well the first spring in at least one of the plantings, and the cultivars outperformed the species that were included. A strong showing the first spring did not guarantee a repeat performance the second and third years. In general, all cultivars deteriorated over time with a noticeable decrease in flower size and vigor. With few exceptions all bulbs planted at the lower depth of 20 cm (8 in.) survived the winters better and outperformed those planted

TABLE 1.

Classification of tulips

Division I	Single Early	Next to species types in time of flowering; moderate height 25 to 40 cm (10 to 15 in.) (e.g., Bellona, Couleur Cardinal, Princess Irene)
Division II	Double Early	Similar to single early varieties, but flowers are longer lasting. Useful for indoor forcing (e.g., Carlton, Peach Blossom)
Division III	Triumphs	Developed by crossing single early and Darwin varieties. Flower about 10 days earlier than Darwins and are much larger and taller than single earlies [50-60 cm (20 to 24 in.) tall] (e.g., Paul Richter)
Division IV	Darwin Hybrids	Long slender stems, huge globular flowers in wide range of colors (lower part of flower often rectangular in outline) (e.g., Apeldoorn, Big Chief, Elizabeth Arden)
Division V	Cottage and Darwin (Single Late)	Long flexible stems, flowers often egg shaped with long pointed petals, clear brilliant colors (e.g., Ivory Glory, Aristocrat, Clara Butt)
Division VI	Lily-Flowered	Long pointed recurving petals originated by crossing *T. retroflexa* with other tulips (e.g., Queen of Sheba, Marietta, West Point)
Division VII	Fringed	Tulips with crystal shaped fringes on the tips and edges of the tepals (e.g., Radiant Apogee, Fringed Apeldoorn, Frosty Dawn)
Division VIII	Viridiflora	Includes the species *Tulipa viridiflora* and its hybrids. These plants are characterized by having large, light green tepals, usually yellow colored at their margins. Often described as bizarre (e.g., Greenland, Artist)
Division IX	Rembrandt	Broken or variegated Darwin tulips (e.g., Cordell Hull, Montgomery, American Flag)
Division X	Parrots	Mostly mutants of well-known garden varieties. Have laciniated, twisted petals, often with green markings. Flowers large (e.g., Fantasy, Blue Parrot, White Parrot, Orange Favorite)
Division XI	Peony Flowered (Double Late)	These are more accurately double triumphs which bloom with earlier Darwins (e.g., Eros, Mount Tacoma, Uncle Tom)
Division XII	*T. kaufmanniana*	Includes both the species and its cultivars and hybrids. Known as the water lily tulip; early flowering. Native to mountains of Turkestan.
Division XIII	*T. fosteriana*	Includes both the species and its cultivars and hybrids. Very large, brilliant scarlet flowers exemplify the species. Its cultivar 'Red Emperor' is perhaps the best known. Flowers slightly later than *T. kaufmanniana* but also native to Turkestan.
Division XIV	*T. greigii*	Includes both the species and its cultivars and hybrids. A native of Turkestan that usually flowers later than *T. fosteriana*. A handsome plant with finely mottled leaves.
Division XV	Other species including *T. praestans, T. tarda, T. kolpakowskiana, T. urumiensis*	A miscellaneous category that includes some species that are well adapted to the prairie climate.

FIGURE 67a. *Tulipa* 'Mount Tacoma'

FIGURE 67b. *Tulipa* 'Gudoshnik'

FIGURE 67c. *Tulipa* 'Ivory Glory'

FIGURE 67d. *Tulipa* 'Mariette'

FIGURE 67e. *Tulipa* 'Greenland'

FIGURE 67f. *Tulipa tarda*

FIGURE 67g. *Tulipa tarda*

FIGURE 67h. *Tulipa urumiensis*

only 10 cm (4 in.) deep. The shallow planted bulbs were often heaved out of the ground by frost action. Furthermore, the replacement bulbs produced each spring would reach the surface by the third season.

What this project did illustrate is that tulip cultivars, regardless of division, with the possible exception of the parrots (Division X), can perform satisfactorily the first spring after planting if good quality bulbs are planted and the soil is properly prepared to allow for deep planting with good drainage. Although none of the species tulips included in the test did particularly well, the most hardy species such as *Tulipa tarda* and *Tulipa kolpakowskiana* were not included. Both of these perform well in the prairie region, and actually will multiply and spread over time.

A fairly recent tulip trial in Calgary, Alberta, Canada, confirms the variability that can occur among cultivars. Single early and Darwin cultivars as groups (Divisions I and IV) were the most successful in large display beds providing long lasting, effective and colorful shows. The species types, including their cultivars, proved satisfactory in small pocket plantings or microclimatic niches.

In general, Darwins are the most popular on the Canadian prairies because they bloom late and thereby miss late spring frosts. Protection in the form of heavy snow cover or a good mulch during severe winter weather is considered important in most areas. Of the species tulips tested at the Agriculture and Agri-Food Canada Research Station in Manitoba, *Tulipa tarda* and *Tulipa kolpakowskiana* were rated fully hardy and capable of being maintained over long periods of time without special care. Recent trials have added *Tulipa turkistanica* and *Tulipa urumiensis* to the list of hardy, good performance species.

For Saskatchewan, the survey indicated that cultivars of single early, Darwin and single late (cottage) were the most satisfactory. Single earlies can be a problem if planted where they will come up too early and be injured by late hard frosts. Again *Tulipa tarda* and *Tulipa kolpakowskiana* were the most successful species being grown.

Ed Toop

University of Alberta Plant Science Collection

FIGURE 69.

Tulipa tarda.

Tulipa kolpakowskiana

A native of Central Asia, the bulb is medium sized and broadly **ovoid** with a dark brown tunic (outer scale). Each stem has three leaves near its base, **linear** to **lanceolate** and upright, with a slight waxy bloom and 10 to 15 cm (4 to 6 in.) in length. Stems are slender, bright green, 25 to 35 cm (10 to 14 in.) in height; the flowers are erect, widely bell-shaped, medium-sized, normally yellow, but often reddish or greenish externally. It is a very attractive plant and very hardy, but appears to require dry baked soil conditions during the summer rest period.

Tulipa tarda

A native of eastern Turkestan or the Trans-Ilian Ala Tau mountains, the bulb is globe shaped, 2.5 cm (1 in.) in diameter with the tunic prolonged into a neck. The leaves (up to seven) are either alternate or opposite, lance-shaped or linear, dull green and 15 to 23 cm (6 to 9 in.) in length; the stems are erect, 5 to 8 cm (2 to 3 in.) long; there are 2 to 7 flowers, erect or slightly nodding, eventually widely expanded, yellow and white, with tepals up to 5 cm (2 in.) in length. This plant has long been grown in gardens as *Tulipa dasystemon*. It is very floriferous and excellent for rock gardens.

DAFFODILS

The common name "daffodil" is associated in most people's minds with the yellow flowered narcissus, having a well-developed trumpet or **corona**. However, this is only one type of a rather diverse group of species and cultivars within the genus *Narcissus*. The genus is indigenous to only the northern hemisphere with the main habitat ranging from Switzerland south through Portugal and North Africa and north through Europe to north of the British Isles. Much breeding work was done in Britain during the 19th century to develop the wide range of cultivars available today. Like the tulips, the daffodils have been classified into divisions based on genetic background, growth habit and flower characteristics (see Table 2).

Daffodils should be planted in late August or early September, but often bulbs are not available until late September or early October. With ample moisture available and warm soil temperature at the time of planting, the bulbs will develop an extensive root system which is essential for their emergence as strong flowering plants in the spring. Late planted bulbs that do not develop this root system prior to winter will have scant foliage and small flowers on short stems if flower stalks emerge at all the following spring. The ideal situation

TABLE 2.
Classification of daffodils

Division I	Trumpet	Corona as long or longer than perianth segments. There is one flower per stem.
Division II	Large Cupped	Corona more than one third but less than equal to length of perianth segments. There is one flower per stem.
Division III	Small Cupped	Corona not more than one-third length of perianth segments. There is one flower per stem.
Division IV*	Double	Double flower types.
Division V	Triandrus	*N. triandrus* and its hybrids. Rush-like leaves, flowers 1 to 6 per stem, white with cup-like corona.
Division VI	Cyclamineus	*N. cyclamineus* and its hybrids. Single flowers drooping or nodding, perianth yellow, segments **reflexed**.
Division VII	Jonquilla	*N. jonquilla* and its hybrids. Leaves rush-like to 45 cm (18 in.), yellow fragrant flowers, 2 to 6 per stem. Corona less than half the length of the perianth segments and wavy edged.
Division VIII	Tazetta	*N. tazetta* (Poetaz) and its hybrids. Fragrant white flowers 4 to 8 per stem, light yellow coronas. Paper white narcissus has white corona.
Division IX	Poeticus	*N. poeticus* and its hybrids without admixture of any other group. Flowers usually solitary, white, fragrant with red-edged, flat, waved yellow corona much shorter than perianth segments.
Division X	Species and wild forms	Most pleasing for naturalizing under shrubs and for use in rock gardens. For more information on small sized species, see *Hardy Bulbs I* by E G Anderson listed in the Reference section.
Division XI	Miscellaneous	Narcissi not falling into any of the above divisions.

Divisions I, II, III, V, VI and VII have subdivisions based on color and length of corona.

*In some listings, Division IV is called the Leedsi Group: corona white or pale citron, sometimes tinged with pink or apricot, perianth white.

FIGURE 70a. *Narcissus* 'Signal Light'

FIGURE 70b. *Narcissus* sp.

FIGURE 70a. *Narcissus* sp.

TABLE 3.

Crocuses that succeed on the prairies

*C. ancyrensis**	Rich orange from Turkey
C. chrysanthus and varieties	White, cream, yellow, orange, and blue blossoms from Greece and Turkey
C. alativicus	White blooms with yellow throat, exterior of outer segments speckled purple from Ala-Tau mountains of Russia
*C. speciosus*** and varieties	Pale to deep violet blue blooms from Russia, Turkey and Iran
*C. kotschyanus*** (*C. zonatus*)	Pale rosy lilac with orange spots at base; indigenous to Lebanon and Turkey
C. dalmaticus	Rose pink, bluish violet blooms from coastal mountains of Croatia
C. etruscus	Rose pink, bluish blooms from Italy
C. susianus	Deep golden yellow with mahogany stripes; indigenous to southern Russia
C. tomasinianus and varieties	Pale lavender to red purple blooms from Dalmatia
*C. longiflorus***	Pale lilac purple striped blooms from Italy and Sicily
Winter flowering (November to February) and spring flowering are all spring flowering in our climate. * Winter flowering ** Fall flowering	

involves rapid root development accompanied by slight leaf emergence through the apex of the bulb within two to three weeks after planting (see Figure 66). Once this has happened, further development will not occur until spring since the bulbs must be subjected to several weeks of cold temperatures in order to trigger future growth.

Daffodils will grow in a wide range of soil types, but are best in a deep clay loam that is slightly acidic. It should be a well-drained site that can be kept fairly dry during the summer rest period. *Narcissus poeticus* and its hybrids have a very short summer rest period and will thrive in low moist ground unsuited to other types. South or east facing slopes offer good drainage for encouraging early uniform development and a better show of color.

CROCUSES

To the prairie dweller the name crocus is often synonymous with prairie crocus, a hardy native plant with the scientific name *Anemone patens*. This is not a bulb forming plant and is not even related to the true crocus. The *Crocus* produces a corm rather than a bulb as its storage organ. Unfortunately, the most popular members of the genus *Crocus* are not hardy in the prairie climate. However, there are a number of crocus species indigenous to such areas as Turkey, Russia, and Iran that have been successfully grown in the prairie region. Some of these species are either fall-flowering or winter-flowering in their native habitats, but will flower in the spring if planted in regions where winter comes early.

Table 3 lists crocus species that have been tried with some success in Alberta, Canada.

Other genera related to crocus that produce crocus-like flowers are *Colchicum* and *Bulbocodium*. Species of these genera tend to produce their flowers well in advance of the

FIGURE 71a. Crocus sp.

FIGURE 71b. *Crocus chrysanthus* 'Blue Pearl'

FIGURE 72a. *Bulbocodium vernum*

FIGURE 72b. *Bulbocodium vernum*

FIGURE 73. *Chionodoxa gigantea*

FIGURE 74. *Scilla sibirica* 'Spring Beauty'

FIGURE 75a. *Puschkinia libanotica*

FIGURE 75b. *Puschkinia scilloides*

foliage and often bloom in the autumn. The species *Bulbocodium vernum* has bloomed and multiplied successfully at the University of Alberta Devonian Botanic Garden and in several urban gardens across the Canadian prairies. It blooms in early spring with rosy mauve flowers, white spotted on the exterior with one to three blooms per bulb. The rather broad channelled leaves appear after the blooms fade.

SQUILLS

Squills make attractive ribbon plantings or small groupings as well as attractive additions to a rock garden. They perform best in full sun with good drainage. They easily self-propagate from both seed and bulb offsets.

Another closely related genus to the squills is *Chionodoxa* or glory of the snow. The chief species grown is *Chionodoxa lucliae* which produces blue white-centred flowers on stems 8 to 15 cm (3 to 6 in.) tall.

Siberian squills or bluebells (*Scilla sibirica*) have delicate nodding blue flowers in May and are about 15 cm (6 in.) in height. There is a pure white form called *Scilla sibirica* 'Alba', a deeper blue slightly taller cultivar called 'Spring Beauty', and a brighter blue variety called *Scilla sibirica taurica*, all of which are fully hardy.

Striped squills (*Puschkinia libanotica* or *P. scilloides*) are very similar to the Siberian squill, but have white flowers striped with blue. A pure white form (*P. libanotica alba*) is also available.

GRAPE HYACINTHS

These plants are members of the genus *Muscari* of which there are many species; most are very similar in appearance. The two hardiest species appear to be *Muscari armeniacum* and *Muscari botryoides*. The former produces erect stems 20 to 23 cm (8 to 9 in.) in height with grape-like clusters of bright blue flowers; the latter is very similar with height ranging from 15 to 25 cm (6 to 10 in.). *Muscari armeniacum* is often listed as 'Heavenly Blue' because of its sky blue color. In addition to blue, there are also white and pink forms of *Muscari botryoides*.

FIGURE 76. *Muscari armeniacum*

FIGURE 77a. *Fritillaria pudica*

FIGURE 77b. *Fritillaria pallidiflora*

FIGURE 78. *Ixiolirion* sp.

FIGURE 79a. *Allium schoenoprasum*

FIGURE 79b. *Allium schoenoprasum*

FRITILLARY

The widely advertised crown imperial (*Fritillaria imperialis*) is not hardy in the prairie region. However, the Siberian fritillary (*Fritillaria pallidiflora*) is not only perfectly hardy but soon multiplies. These are plants with soft yellow nodding flowers on stems 23 cm (9 in.) in height produced in early spring. The species *Fritillaria meleagris*, known under the various common names of snake's head, checkered lily, or guinea hen fritillary, can also be successfully grown if guaranteed good snow cover through the coldest part of the winter. Its drooping, petite, graceful, marbled blooms range in color from purple to silvery-grey on 30 cm (1 ft.) stems. *Fritillaria pudica* is hardy and similar to the Siberian fritillary but somewhat shorter.

IXIOLIRION

Ixiolirions produce a tuft of narrow grass-like leaves. The lavender-blue flowers, about 4 cm (1.5 in.) in length, are produced in clusters on slender stems 30 cm (1 ft.) in length in late June. They are rather rare but easily grown and perfectly hardy.

ALLIUMS OR FLOWERING ONIONS

The genus *Allium* brings to mind culinary species such as garlic, chives, leeks, and the common onion. Among these, chives (*Allium schoenoprasum*) can also serve as a very attractive ornamental plant. There are also a number of other species of *Allium* that are very showy, hardy and easily grown. They are useful for planting in a wild flower garden or among hardy ferns where their **umbels** or globe-like flower clusters bearing blooms of various colors are

FIGURE 80. *Allium caeruleum*

FIGURE 81. *Allium oreophilum*

FIGURE 82. *Allium moly*

attractive in spring and summer. Some of the smaller kinds make excellent rock garden plants. The bulbs can be planted in the fall or early spring in a sunny location.

Blue globe onion (*Allium caeruleum* syn. *Allium azureum*), a native to Siberia, reaches 60 cm (2 ft.) in height and produces deep blue flowers in 5 cm (2 in.) diameter globes in June.

Ostrowsky onion (*Allium oreophilum* syn. *Allium ostrowskianum*) is a native of Turkestan and an excellent bulb for the rock garden. Only 15 cm (6 in.) tall, it produces soft pink flowers in June.

Golden garlic (*Allium moly*), a native of the French and Spanish Pyrenees , produces lovely golden flower heads on 30 cm (1 ft.) stems in June.

Naples onion (*Allium neapolitanum* syn. *Allium cowanii*) produces delightfully fragrant white star-like flowers on 30 cm (1 ft.) stems in May.

LILIES

The most popular flowering bulb for the prairie region is the hardy lily. In addition to many *Lilium* species, there are a multitude of hardy hybrid cultivars, many of which were developed on the Canadian prairies; some of these are Patterson hybrids, Honeywood hybrids, and Dropmore hybrids. Many plants are called lilies, but all true lilies are classified under the genus *Lilium*. They all produce an **imbricate bulb.**

Lilies, unlike most other bulbs, do not go into a dormancy after flowering, but continue to make root growth as long as conditions of moisture and temperature are favorable. If dug prematurely, the bulbs do not keep well out of the ground. For this reason, many growers are not able to ship lily bulbs until late September or early October. This date still gives enough time for the root growth and development needed to anchor the plant before the onset of winter. Because new growth begins so early in the spring, do not move lilies then, since young shoots or sprouts are so easily broken. If a sprout is broken off in handling, that bulb will not grow again until it has gone through another winter or simulated winter environmental conditions.

Because lily bulbs have no real period of dormancy and have fleshy roots and no protective outer tunic, they should be replanted as soon as possible after digging. It is important to keep moist packing material around each

FIGURE 83a. *Lilium* sp.

FIGURE 83b. *Lilium philidelphicum*

FIGURE 84a. Up-facing
Lilium 'Earli Bird'

FIGURE 84b. Out-facing *Lilium*

FIGURE 84c. Down-facing
Lilium 'Honey Queen'

bulb during the handling and merchandising process to prevent desiccation of these fleshy roots and bulb scales.

A spring planted lily bulb usually will not grow as tall or carry as many blooms as one of the same size and variety planted the previous fall. However, with newly perfected storage methods, lily bulbs may be carried through winter in excellent condition and shipped for spring planting as firm and crisp as if they had been freshly dug.

Most lilies are best planted or replanted in the fall, but those of marginal hardiness are more likely to acclimatize and survive if planted in the spring.

Like the tulips and daffodils, lilies have also been categorized into various divisions. Those grown in cold climates and considered hardy with little or no added protection generally fall into one of three categories: Asiatic hybrids, martagon hybrids, or selected species. With additional care and protection, some of the more tender trumpet and aurelian lilies can be successfully grown.

Asiatic Hybrids

As the name implies, the species lilies from which this group was derived came originally from Asia. Most are easy to grow and flower quite early. They have a broad color range, but most are unscented. The Patterson hybrids, developed at the University of Saskatchewan, Saskatoon, Canada, by the late Dr. C F Patterson, are among these and were

developed from parentage including *Lilium cernuum*, *L. davidii*, *L. davidii* var. *willmottiae* and *L. tigrinum*. Within the Asiatics there are three classes:

Class A:
Up-facing flowers, very showy, good as cut blooms.

Class B:
Out-facing flowers, more blooms per stem than class "A" hybrids, thus often providing a longer season of color. Good as cut flowers.

Class C:
Down-facing or pendant flowers, these carry the most blooms of the Asiatics. Graceful and very impressive, especially when massed in groups.

Martagon or Martagon-Hansonii Hybrids
These tall lilies with many small **turkscap blossoms** and **whorled leaves** (leaves attached in "wheels" or whorls around the stem at well-spaced nodes) are very stately and decorative. Yellow, white, pink, lavender, light orange and deep dark red are the most common colors, often with speckles or freckle markings.

Species Lilies
These are the wild lilies found by plant explorers throughout the northern hemisphere and have been used to breed all the hybrids

FIGURE 85a. *Lilium amabile*

FIGURE 85b. *Lilium dauricum*

FIGURE 85c. *Lilium tsingtauense*

known today. They vary considerably in height, color and form. Some of the species that are winter hardy include *L. amabile, L. cernuum, L. dauricum, L. davidii, L. tigrinum* and *L. tsingtauense.* It is from these lilies that plant breeders have created the magnificent hardy hybrids. Yet species lilies, themselves, often possess a delicate charm that appeals to many people. It is not only because hybridizers believe that they are improving on the species that they cross and recross these lilies, but also because they can expand the variety of flower color, height, shape and/or season of bloom. As well, they can incorporate hybrid vigor to produce plants that are better suited to our garden conditions. True species often decline under domestication in our gardens, but hybrids thrive on it.

Although the Asiatics, martagons and several hardy species are the most commonly grown lilies on the prairies, some of the semi-hardy and even tender cultivars such as the aurelian and trumpet lilies have been successful for lily fanciers. They are usually tall and fragrant and may require staking. They generally also require mulching to prevent hard frosts from nipping the emerging buds. Tender types should be planted in the spring rather than the fall to give them one growing season to acclimatize. Once established, they may often winter well for several years in sheltered locations.

FIGURE 86.

Lilium 'Rosalinda'

FIGURE 87.
Trumpet lily hybrid

PERENNIALS FOR THE PLAINS AND PRAIRIES

FIGURE 88a. *Lilium* 'Rose Dawn'

FIGURE 88b. *Lilium* 'Redland'

FIGURE 88c. *Lilium* 'Ruby'

FIGURE 88d. *Lilium* 'Sunbright'

FIGURE 88e. *Lilium* 'Lemon Queen'

FIGURE 88f. *Lilium* 'Red Torch'

FIGURE 88g. *Lilium* 'Fuchsia Queen'

FIGURE 88h. *Lilium* 'Amulet'

Plant descriptions

How to use this section

The descriptions of the specific plants dealt with in this section are accompanied by the icons illustrated here to allow the reader to see at a glance the general height of each species or group of hybrids, the sunlight requirements and soil moisture requirements. The individual requirements for each perennial cannot be accurately depicted by these icons but they do help in categorizing the plants according to average height and the environmental conditions under which they should thrive. More detailed and accurate information is given in the text and in the reference charts.

 Low, mat-forming, edging or foreground material up to 45 cm (18 in.) tall.

 Medium height, middleground and shorter background material 50 to 110 cm (2 to 3.5 ft.) tall.

 Low to medium height material which overlaps the foreground middleground height range.

 Tall background material 120 to 180 cm (4 to 6 ft.).

 Full sun

 Partial shade

 Full sun to partial shade

 Full shade

 Requires moist or evenly moist soil conditions

 Requires dry soil or is drought resistant

Achillea spp.
Yarrow

Introduction: Yarrows are a group of perennials characterized by their drought tolerance and ability to naturalize or fill a space quickly by means of spreading underground stolons. Most do better in poor rather than rich soils, in full sun.

Achillea filipendulina
Fernleaf Yarrow

Description: Flat heads of yellow flowers are produced on 1 to 1.3m (3 to 4 ft.) stems among fern-like foliage blooming from July to September.

Many of the cultivars such as 'Coronation Gold', 'Gold Plate', and 'Parker's Variety' have not been extensively tested in the prairie climate and may require a more sheltered location. 'Cloth of Gold' has not proved hardy under severe winter conditions.

Culture: They do best in well drained soils in full sun.

Use: The fernleaf yarrow is massed toward the back of the border and used as a cut flower in fresh or dried arrangements. If using as an everlasting, cut prior to pollen development for best color retention.

Propagation: Seed will produce plants with a great deal of variation, which may not be true to type. Seed germinates readily at 20°C (70°F). Propagation is also through cuttings and division.

Achillea filipendulina 'Coronation Gold'

Achillea filipendulina

Achillea millefolium 'Cerise Queen'

Achillea - mixed planting

Achillea millefolium
Common Yarrow

Description: Characterized by aromatic, finely divided leaves and tiny white flowers, common yarrow is considered a naturalized weed introduced from Europe and Asia. Some of its cultivars, however, have been developed for the perennial border.

'Cerise Queen' has rosy-pink flowers and fern-like, dark green foliage and is 45 to 60 cm (18 to 24 in.) in height, blooming in July and August.

Another cultivar, 'Fire King', is similar but with deep carmine flowers. It has not been widely tested in severe climates but should be worthy of trial.

Culture: They do best in full sun and well-drained soil and are drought tolerant once established. They "naturalize" quickly so will need some control to prevent them from becoming weedy.

Use: They are excellent massed in the border and in fresh or dried arrangements.

Propagation: Propagation is by seed (expect some variation: colors will range from cream to deep red), division, cuttings, or stolons.

Achillea ptarmica 'The Pearl'

Achillea ptarmica
Sneezewort

Description: Sneezewort blooms in July and August with a myriad of tiny, double, pure white flowers on 45 to 60 cm (18 to 24 in.) stems. The double form, now considered standard, has been in existence since the 1500s. 'The Pearl' (originally called Boule de Neige or Snowball) has button-like flowers in branching heads.

Culture: Like other yarrows, they grow in full sun and well drained soil.

Use: Sneezeworts are useful as cut or dried flowers and for softening color clashes among pinks, reds, and oranges. Include them in a "night garden" or a border devoted to whites and greys.

Propagation: Propagation is similar to other yarrows.

Achillea ptarmica

Achillea tomentosa
Woolly Yarrow

Description: A dwarf plant of 8 to 10 cm (3 to 4 in.), woolly yarrow is characterized by woolly, grey, finely cut foliage and yellow flowers in June.

Culture: Plant in full sun in well-drained soil.

Use: Useful in the rock garden (along with thymes, alyssum, dwarf veronicas and bellflowers), toward the front of a perennial border, as groundcover, and for interplanting among paving stones toward the edge of a walkway or patio.

Propagation: Propagation is by division.

Ed Toop

Achillea tomentosa

Alberta Horticultural Association

Achillea tomentosa

Aconitum napellus

Ed Toop

Gail Rankin

Aconitum napellus 'Bicolor'

Aconitum napellus
Monkshood

Description: Monkshood is a stately, 1 to 1.5 m (3 to 4 ft.) perennial with glossy, finely divided, dark green foliage and spikes of purple flowers with hooded petals, blooming in July. *A. napellus* 'Bicolor' has white flowers edged with blue but is otherwise similar. All plant parts are poisonous, the tuberous roots especially so.

Culture: They grow best in deep, evenly moist, organic soil in partial shade. Monkshood will grow in full sun as long as moisture is not a limiting factor. (If subject to full sun and droughty conditions, the leaves may "burn," appearing black as though diseased.)

Use: Because of their height, they are best planted toward the back of the border. They are also useful as cut flowers. They are sometimes used in semi-wild gardens where shade and moisture are abundant.

Propagation: Monkshood are easily propagated by division in early spring. They are more difficult by seed. Older seed is generally non-viable and even fresh seed will show sporadic germination.

Adonis vernalis
Spring Adonis

Description: One of the earliest perennials to bloom, the spring adonis produces buttercup-like, yellow flowers on 30cm (12in.) stems in May. The foliage is delicate and fern-like. By July the foliage has all but disappeared, to return again the following spring. (This is a perennial which might be worth labeling to avoid accidentally digging it up.)

Culture: Grow in sun or partial shade in loamy soils.

Use: Adonis are well suited to planting in "drifts," both for the fullest impact of color in the early spring, and because they will virtually disappear by mid-summer.

Sara Wiliams

Adonis vernalis

They are useful in both the semi-shaded wild garden and the rockery.

Propagation: Like other members of the buttercup family (Ranunculaceae), even fresh seed germinates unevenly. Careful division in early spring is recommended.

Aegopodium podagraria 'Variegatum'
Bishop's Goutweed

Description: Valued for its variegated leaves and ability to survive adverse conditions, goutweed should be accompanied by a Surgeon General's warning which might read: "Plant only where its rampant growth can be restricted" (e.g., between a cement sidewalk and a house). Once believed to cure gout, hence its common name, it is grown for its green and yellow to cream-colored foliage of 30 to 38 cm (12 to 15 in.) in height rather than its taller umbels of rather insignificant flowers. It will occasionally revert to the green leaf species type. Such shoots should be removed.

Culture: It grows equally well in sun or shade in almost any soil type. If it appears untidy or rangy, it may be mowed.

Use: Goutweed makes an excellent, fast-growing ground cover, especially useful as an understory below trees or shrubs. It should not be planted in a rock garden or perennial border as it will soon choke out more choice material.

Propagation: Propagation is by stolons or division.

Aegopodium podograria 'Variegatum'

Aegopodium podograria

Ajuga reptans

Olds College Collection

Ajuga reptans *'Multicolor'*

Gail Rankin

Ajuga reptans
Carpet Bugleweed

Description: Bugleweed forms a mat-like ground cover of bronzy green, basal leaves of 15 cm (6 in.) in height, above which are carried short spikes of blue flowers in June. Some cultivars have variegated leaves. These will need shade to bring out the variegation. Variegated forms are not as hardy and may not survive in some prairie areas (check with local nurseries).

Culture: It will grow in either partial or full shade with even moisture. In full sun there may be danger of sun scald in early spring. (It may winterkill during an unusual winter with alternate thawing and freezing or where snow cover is inadequate.)

Use: Excellent as a groundcover or underplanting below trees and shrubs, carpet bugleweed is also useful in a rock garden or as edging material.

Propagation: Frequent division is necessary to prevent over-crowding. Propagate in spring by division.

Ajuga reptans

Alcea rosea
Hollyhock

History: There are several derivations of the common name. Although the plant is a native of China, introduced to Europe in the 1500s, many believed it was from the Holyland. Thus, one derivation of the name became "holy hock." As well, the leaves were once used to reduce the swelling on the hocks of horses.

Description: An old fashioned garden favorite, hollyhocks are available in shades of pink, yellow, red, maroon and white, blooming in July and August on 2m (6 ft.) stalks.

Although they are sometimes more difficult to obtain, the single varieties have proved hardier than the double but even these are not long-lived. Because hollyhocks are available as annuals, biennials, and perennials and have a habit of self-seeding, it can be difficult to determine just which type one has!

Culture: They do well in rich soils with good drainage in full sun. Rust and spider mites can sometimes be problems. They may need to be staked.

Use: Because of their stature, they are best planted at the back of the border.

Propagation: Hollyhocks are easily raised from seed and beds perpetuate themselves by reseeding.

Althaea rosea

Saskatchewan Department of Agriculture & Food

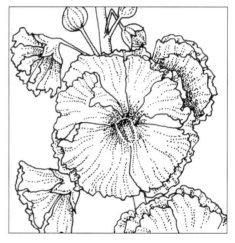

Althaea rosea

Anchusa azurea
Italian Bugloss

Description: Anchusa is a semi-erect plant of 1 to 1.3 m (3 to 4 ft.) with coarse, hairy leaves and bright blue flowers, 2 cm (0.75 in.) in diameter, blooming in June and July. It tends to be rather short-lived under prairie conditions but might be worth growing for the intensity of its blue flowers.

Culture: It does best in full sun in soil which is moist but well-drained.

Use: Bugloss is perhaps best suited for a semi-wild garden where it can be naturalized en masse and its floppy habit will not be offensive. In a border it will require staking.

Propagation: Propagation is by seed, division, or root cuttings.

Anchusa azurea

Anemone pulsatilla

Anemone pulsatilla

Anemone pulsatilla (Pulsatilla vulgaris)
European Pasque Flower

Description: A close relative of the native American or prairie pasque flower (*A. patens*), which is often referred to as the "Prairie Crocus," the European pasque flower is very similar in appearance, but carries larger flowers of a more intense color, often deep purple or wine colored. At 22 to 38 cm (9 to 15 in.) in height, the pasque flower is among the first perennials to bloom in the spring. The grey-green leaves are finely divided and covered with silky hairs. The silky seed pods which follow the flowers are also of ornamental value.

Culture: Pasque flowers prefer a well-drained, sunny location.

Use: Because of their short stature they are best used in the rock garden or toward the front of the border.

Propagation: Propagation is by seed, division, or root cuttings. Division and root cuttings should be carried out in the spring.

Anemone sylvestris
Snowdrop Anemone

Description: A spreading plant of 30 to 38 cm (12 to 15 in.) with dark green leaves, the snowdrop anemone produces nodding, pure white, scented 5 cm (2 in.) flowers in May and June and may flower again in fall.

Culture: They grow equally well in sun or shade in most soils, but perform better under conditions of even moisture.

Use: Because they self-seed, these anemones are well suited for naturalizing under trees and shrubs, but may also be used as edging, and for the shady or wild garden. Within a more formal border, their spreading habit would have to be controlled.

Propagation: Anemones spread by underground stems and are easily divided in early spring. They also self-seed.

Anemone sylvestris

Anemone sylvestris

Antennaria rosea
Pussytoes

Description: A native of the prairies, pussytoes forms a low, woolly, grey-green mat of 5 to 7 cm (2 to 3 in.), with pink flower heads rising to about 15 to 20 cm (6 to 8 in.). A white species (*Antennaria aprica*) is more common in the wild. Both flower in June and July.

Culture: They grow best in well-drained soil in full sun and are extremely drought tolerant.

Antennaria rosea

Antennaria rosea

Use: Pussytoes are excellent in a rock garden or among paving stones. They are also useful as an everlasting.

Propagation: Propagation is by division in spring or by seed.

Anthemis tinctoria

Sara Williams

Anthemis tinctoria

Gail Rankin

Anthemis tinctoria
Camomile or Golden Marguerite

Description: A yellow daisy with flowers 2.5 cm (1 in.) in diameter, camomile blooms in June and July on 60 cm (2 ft.) stems above the dark green, finely-divided, aromatic foliage. 'Kelwayi' has deep yellow flowers while 'Moonlight' has pale yellow flowers.

Culture: This perennial thrives in hot dry soil and full sun.

Use: It is useful in a wild garden or a hot dry area or bank where it can be readily "naturalized". It self-seeds too readily for the more fastidious gardener. It is also useful as a cut flower. Older flowering stems can be cut down to encourage new basal growth.

Propagation: Camomile is easily propagated by seed or division and, once established, self-seeds readily.

Aquilegia spp.
Columbine

Description: The columbine is an old-fashioned, but sometimes short-lived, perennial with graceful foliage and spurred flowers in May and June. Heights range from 20 cm to 1 m (8 in. to 3 ft.) and flower colors include white, yellow, pink, red, purple, and blue.

Most of the species and hybrids have proven hardy. The long-spurred hybrids such as 'McKana' and 'Mrs Scott Elliot' are well adapted to the prairies. Both include mixed colors and are about 75 cm (30 in.) high. The American columbine (*A. canadensis*) is 60 cm (2 ft.) high with nodding red and yellow flowers and short spurs. The Colorado or Rocky Mountain columbine (*A. caerulea*) is 30 cm (1 ft.) high with blue and white flowers. The alpine columbine (*A. alpina*) is also 30 cm (1 ft.) high with deep blue flowers and dark green leaves.

Culture: Columbines grow best in moist, well-drained, organically enriched soil in full sun or partial shade.

They are sometimes attacked by leaf miners as well as stem borers. The leaf miner makes its presence known by winding trails of white inside the leaf. Removing infected leaves and cleaning up dead foliage in the fall will help control leaf miners. Powdery mildew can also be a problem where air circulation is poor. Sulfur is the recommended control.

Use: Columbines look equally well in the perennial border, the shade garden, or a wild garden. The dwarf species and cultivars may be utilized in the rock garden.

Propagation: They are easily raised from seed, but may not bloom their first year. Columbines self-sow readily but hybridize so easily that these seedlings are seldom true. Smaller plants may be carefully divided in early spring. This is more difficult as the plants become larger.

Aquilegia alpina

Aquilegia

Aquilegia canadensis

Arabis alpina

Alberta Horticultural Association

Arabis alpina
Rockcress

Description: Dwarf and prostrate, rockcress is an early (May) flowering perennial of 15 to 20 cm (6 to 8 in.) with masses of tiny white or pink flowers which practically conceal the soft grey foliage. It forms a mat of 30 to 38 cm (12 to 15 in.) diameter.

Culture: Rockcress requires full sun and good drainage and tends to be fairly drought resistant. For a neater appearance, cut back or shear the spent flowers after blooming. If snow cover is inadequate in early spring, some browning and dieback might occur.

Use: As well as a rockery plant, rockcress is ideal for the front of the perennial border. Plant near a patio or walk to enjoy its fragrance.

Propagation: It is easily raised from seed, division, or root cuttings.

Arabis caucasica

Olds College Collection

Arabis caucasica (A. albida)
Wall Rockcress

Description: Wall rockcress differs from *A. alpina* in that the flowers are in looser racemes. Otherwise, culture, use, and propagation are similar. 'Snowcap' is a single white flowered cultivar. There appears to be some confusion between *Arabis alpina* and *Arabis caucasica*.

Culture: Wall rockcress requires full sun and good drainage and tends to be fairly drought resistant. For a neater appearance, cut back or shear the spent flowers after blooming. If snow cover is inadequate in early spring, some browning and dieback might occur.

Use: As well as a rockery plant, wall rockcress is ideal for the front of the perennial border. Plant near a patio or walk to enjoy its fragrance.

Propagation: It is easily raised from seed, division, or root cuttings.

Arabis caucasica

Arrhenatherum elatius 'Bulbosum Variegatum'
Tuberous Oatgrass

Description: As the common name implies, this is a tuberous rooted grass which has become naturalized in many parts of North America. Thirty centimetres (1 ft.) in height, it is characterized by variegated bluish-green and white leaves. It is grown for its foliage rather than its flowers which are inconspicuous. Not fully hardy in all areas.

Culture: Oatgrass does well in full sun or partial shade in ordinary, well-drained soil. It is fairly drought tolerant and may be sheared or mowed if it becomes untidy.

Use: It is useful as a specimen plant or in the perennial border.

Propagation: Propagation is by division.

Arrhenatherum elatius 'Bulbosum Variegatum'

Artemisia ludoviciana

Artemisia ludoviciana 'Silver King'
Ghost Plant

Description: A much more aggressive plant than wormwood, ghost plant is 60 to 100 cm (2 to 3 ft.) high with aromatic, silver grey foliage.

Culture: It does well in sandy soils in full sun and will spread very quickly given ideal conditions – a small nursery grown plant grew quietly but determinedly to a 2 m (6 ft.) diameter clump in a single growing season! It is native to western North American and extremely drought tolerant.

Use: 'Silver King'is best used to naturalize an area which cannot be irrigated. The foliage is utilized in dried arrangements.

Propagation: It is easily propagated by division or stem cuttings.

Artemisia schmidtiana 'Silver Mound'
Wormwood

Artemisia schmidtiana 'Silver Mound'

Description: Grown for its foliage, 'Silver Mound' is known for its compact, mound-like form, soft, silvery-grey leaves, and sage-like fragrance. It grows to about 30 cm (12 in.) in height with a spread of 45 cm (18 in.).

Culture: It should be grown in well-drained, infertile soil in full sun. If grown in shade, or with too much moisture or nitrogen fertilizer, it becomes more open and scraggly in appearance. It may be sheared in July to maintain a neater form.

Use: It is excellent toward the front of a perennial border, in the rock garden, for edging, or in a "white" or "night" garden. It is also useful as a foil between otherwise contrasting colors such as pink, orange, or red.

Propagation: 'Silver Mound' is most easily propagated by stem cuttings taken in early summer.

Artemisia schmidtiana 'Silver Mound'

Aruncus dioicus (A. sylvester)
Goats' Beard

Description: A tall perennial of 1.3 m (4 ft.) with an equal spread, goat's beard produces panicles of creamy white flowers borne in June and July above compound feathery dark green leaves. It is dioecious, with male and female flowers on separate plants. The male plants are considered more showy. The leaves will often turn bronze in fall. (The flowers are followed by bronze seed pods which can be utilized in flower arrangements.)

The cultivar 'Kneiffii' is shorter with more finely divided foliage.

Culture: Goats' beard is best grown in partial shade with even moisture in soil with a fairly high organic matter content.

Use: It is ideal as a specimen plant or toward the back of a perennial border. (Its size will overwhelm a small garden.)

Propagation: Propagate by division in spring or by seed. Seed (from female plants) will require a period of cold stratification. Male plants will not produce seed.

Aruncus dioicus

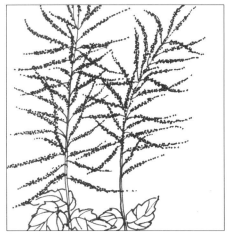

Aruncus dioicus

Aster novae-angliae

Aster

Aster alpinus

Aster spp.
Aster

Description: Most of the asters tested have proven hardy under prairie conditions. Although different species and cultivars may be available locally, the vast majority offered through prairie nurseries are probably worth taking a chance on.

They vary in height from 15 cm to 1 m (6 in. to 3 ft.) and produce daisy-like flowers in white, pink, blue, and shades of red and purple from mid to late summer.

The alpine aster (*Aster alpinus*) is 15 to 25 cm (6 to 10 in.) high with blue or white daisy-like flowers in July. Although many of the michaelmas daisies (*A. novi-belgii*) are fully hardy, some flower too late for prairie gardens. The New England asters (*A. novae-angliae*) are somewhat similar. Some of the earlier flowering cultivars include:

'Blueboy', 38 cm (15 in.), flowering in September and October with medium blue flowers on compact mounds of foliage.

'Pink Bouquet', also 38 cm (15 in.) with mounds of yellow-centred pink flowers blooming in September.

'Purple Beauty', 90 cm (36 in.) with purple flowers in August.

'Romany', a dwarf aster of 20 to 25 cm (8 to 10 in.) with dense dark blue flowers in September and October.

'Rose Beauty', 90 cm (36 in.), with rose-pink flowers in August.

The Italian aster (*A. amellus*) is 60 cm (24 in.) and produces sky-blue flowers in September.

Culture: Most prefer full sun or partial shade. They do well in most prairie soils.

Use: Asters are ideal border plants. Dwarf varieties are useful in the rock garden. All can be utilized as cut flowers.

Propagation: They are best propagated by division in the spring. Hybrids will seldom come true from seed.

Astilbe chinensis 'Pumila'
Dwarf Chinese Astilbe

Description: Introduced from China in 1892, astilbes spread by stolons to form dense, compact clumps. As the common name implies, these plants are only 30 cm (12 in.) tall, with fluffy pink flowers in July and August borne above deep-green compound leaves.

Culture: Like other astilbes, these do best in partial shade in organic, evenly moist soil, but can tolerate somewhat drier conditions than other astilbes. They may not be hardy in all parts of the prairie region.

Use: The dwarf Chinese astilbe is ideal as a ground cover or edging plant or in the rock garden.

Propagation: Propagate by division in spring or by seed.

Astilbe chinensis 'Davidii'

Astilbe chinensis 'Bridal Veil'

Astilbe thunbergii 'Moerheim'
Moerheim's Astilbe

Description: Astilbes are noted for their finely divided leaves above which are carried plumes of flowers on 60 cm (2 ft.) stems. 'Moerheim' has white flowers in July and can be grown successfully with protection.

Culture: All astilbes require partial shade, rich organic soil, and even moisture to do well - conditions sometimes difficult to provide in prairie gardens. They will appear shabby during hot dry summers and may suffer from spider mites. Under such conditions frequent but gentle spraying of the foliage with a garden hose is recommended. Like the dwarf

Astilbe thunbergii 'Moerheim'

Chinese astilbe, Moerheim's astilbe may not be hardy in all parts of the prairie region.

Use: They are a good plant for the middle of a border where their cultural demands can be met or as a pond or waterside planting. The plumes are excellent as cut flowers.

Propagation: Propagate by division in early spring.

Aurinia saxatilis

Alyssum montanum

Aurinia saxatilis (Alyssum saxatile)
Basket-of-Gold
Perennial Alyssum

Description: Having recently undergone a name change, *Aurinia* is perhaps better known to many gardeners as perennial alyssum. It forms a low, spreading, mound-like plant 25 to 30 cm (10 to 12 in.) high with grey-green foliage covered in a mass of tiny bright gold flowers in May and June. 'Compactum' (also called 'Gold Dust') is more compact than the species.

Culture: It does well in full sun in well-drained soil (shade, abundant moisture, and too much fertilizer will result in sprawling, unattractive plants). It may be trimmed or sheared back after flowering for a neater appearance.

Use: *Aurinia* is ideal for the rock garden or toward the front of the perennial border. It may also be planted among paving stones or patio blocks to soften hard surfaces.

Propagation: It is easily raised from seed. It may also be propagated from stem cuttings.

Alyssum montanum (Mountain Alyssum)

Mountain alyssum, which did not undergo a name change, is similar, but with paler flowers and a more mat-forming habit.

Bergenia cordifolia
Bergenia or Giant Rockfoil

Description: Bergenia produces 30 cm (12 in.) spikes of rosy-purple flowers in May. The leaves are large and handsome and turn a reddish bronze in the fall. *Bergenia crassifolia* is similar with slightly smaller, spoon-shaped leaves and flowers that are held higher above the foliage. Because they are evergreen, they may appear somewhat ragged in early spring, but newer growth soon hides this. It is somewhat reassuring to know that bergenia planted in Florida are usually not as vigorous as those grown in the prairie regions of North America. (It is native to Siberia!)

Culture: A very adaptable perennial, bergenia grows equally well in sun or shade.

Use: It is useful in rock gardens, at the edge of pools and other waterside plantings, toward the front of the perennial border, or as an edging plant.

Propagation: Bergenia is easily propagated by division in early spring or by seed. Seeded plants will take 3 to 4 years to reach flowering size.

Bergenia cordifolia

Bergenia cordifolia

Bergenia crassifolia

Callianthemum angustifolium

Callianthemum angustifolium
Callianthemum

Description: A member of the buttercup family native to central Siberia, this unusual perennial is characterized by scalloped, blue-grey leaves and short-stemmed anemone-like white flowers on 15 cm (6 in.) stems in May and early June. The foliage disappears soon after flowering. It is perfectly hardy in prairie gardens but rarely seen.

Culture: It does best in well-drained, but evenly moist loamy soil in full sun or partial shade.

Use: Because of their low stature, callianthemums are best viewed from close by, in a partially shaded portion of a rock garden or near a patio.

Propagation: Propagation is by seed which is sown immediately after being harvested or by division after flowering.

Caltha palustris

Caltha palustris
Marsh Marigold

History: The genus name "caltha" is a contraction of the Greek word "kalathos," meaning a goblet, and refers to the cup-shaped flowers.

Description: Native to the wetlands of Canada and much of the United States, as well as Europe, the marsh marigold will not flourish under the conditions of a perennial border. Given an ideal habitat, it will produce beautiful, yellow, buttercup-like flowers on 30 cm (1 ft.) stems above heart-shaped leaves in May or June. The entire plant may go dormant and disappear by mid-summer. The double form, 'Flore Pleno', is more showy and seems more tolerant of garden conditions.

Culture: It will grow in full sun or partial shade and although it tolerates moist soil it will do better in wet soil rich in organic matter.

Use: Marsh Marigolds are ideal for ponds, streams, water gardens or naturalizing near marshes or bogs.

Propagation: Propagation is by division before or after flowering.

Caltha palustris

Campanula spp.
Bellflower

Introduction: The bellflowers form a large genus of attractive garden plants, many of which are hardy in the prairie landscape. The word "campanula" is from the Latin, means "little bell" and refers to the characteristic flower shape. Of those tested in central Canada in the 1960s, approximately half proved hardy while the remainder rated "medium hardy" or as surviving "most of the time". In a protected home garden, most of these would be worthwhile taking a chance on. The following species are considered fully hardy.

Campanula carpatica
Carpathian Bellflower

Description: Blue, up-facing bell-shaped flowers, 2.5 to 5 cm (1 to 2 in.) across, are produced during much of June and July above a neat mound of foliage which is 30 cm (12 in.) in height with an equal spread. White cultivars are also available.

Campanula carpatica

More readily available cultivars include 'Blue Clips' with larger flowers on compact 20 cm (8 in.) plants, 'White Clips' which is similar but with white flowers, and 'Wedgewood Blue', only 15 cm (6 in.) tall with sky-blue flowers.

Campanula carpatica

Culture: An adaptable perennial, it does well in sun or partial shade, in average well-drained soil.

Use: Because of its neat appearance and long blooming season, the Carpathian bellflower is excellent in the rock garden, toward the front of the perennial border, or in a shady border. The white forms adapt well to a "night" or "white" garden.

Propagation: Propagation is easy from seed or early spring division. It will self-sow to a limited extent.

Campanula cochlearifolia

Campanula cochleariifolia (C. pusilla)
Creeping Bellflower

Description: A tough miniature, this dwarf bellflower is only 8 to 10 cm (3 to 4 in.) high, producing a myriad of tiny blue or white bells in June and July over bright green leaves.

Culture: It grows well in sun or partial shade in ordinary well-drained garden soil.

Use: The creeping bellflower forms dense mats or colonies and is useful as an edging plant, a ground cover, in the rock garden, among paving stones, in the crevices of garden steps, or to soften the hard surface of a patio. (Simply remove a few of the outer bricks or stones, away from the main traffic flow, and tuck in the plants. The fine roots will spread quickly underground between the bricks or stones.) Once established, it will cascade over walls and rocks.

Propagation: Propagation is easiest by division.

Campanula glomerata
Clustered Bellflower or Danesblood Bellflower

Description: Sixty centimetres (2 ft.) in height, the clustered bellflower produces terminal heads of upward-facing rich purple flowers in June and July. White flowered cultivars are also available. Flowers are also produced within the leaf axils. *Campanula glomerata* 'Acaulis' is of dwarf stature, only 15 cm (6 in.) in height with blue-violet flowers. It is less aggressive than the species.

Culture: It does well in sun or partial shade in most garden soils.

Use: It is very effective when massed in the border but should not be allowed to become over crowded. Because it spreads by stolons, it will need regular division and some control.

Propagation: Propagation is by seed and division.

Campanula glomerata

Campanula persicifolia
Peachleaf Bellflower

Description: More solitary than the above-mentioned species, the peachleaf bellflower is about 75 cm (2.5 ft.) high with outward-facing blue or white flowers produced in June and July. The narrow leaves are said to resemble those of the peach.

Culture: It does well in sun or partial shade in well-drained but evenly moist soils.

Use: The peachleaf bellflower is more showy when planted en masse in the border. Although it is reliably hardy, it is slow to increase in size and is definitely not aggressive.

Propagation: Propagation is from seed, cuttings or division.

Campanula persicifolia

Centaurea montana

Centaurea montana
Mountain Bluet, Perennial Cornflower

Description: With globular, thistle-like flowers similar to those of the annual cornflower or bachelor's button, only larger, the mountain bluet blooms in June with less intensive sporadic flowering for the remainder of the summer. The foliage is grey-green and the plants are about 60 cm (2 ft.) in height.

Culture: It will grow well on most soils in full sun or partial shade and is considered fairly drought-tolerant.

Use: The mountain bluet is used both in the perennial border and as a cut flower.

Propagation: They are easily propagated by seed and will self-sow once established. This might be a disadvantage in a more formal border.

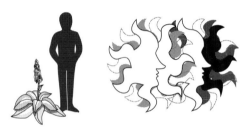

Centaurea montana

Cerastium tomentosum

Cerastium tomentosum
Snow-in-Summer

Description: A low, mat-like creeping plant with silver foliage, snow-in-summer produces tiny white flowers 15 cm (6 in.) high in June.

Culture: It does well in poor soils with good drainage, in full sun. It should be sheared back after flowering for a neater appearance and to keep it from spreading too rampantly.

Use: Although excellent as a ground cover in a hot, dry location, it should be used with caution in a rock garden as it tends to be aggressive.

Propagation: Propagation is by seed, cuttings, or division.

Cerastium tomentosum

Chrysanthemum coccineum
Painted Daisy

History: The insecticide pyrethrum is derived from the flower heads of this plant and was once grown extensively as a cash crop in East Africa. Cheaper, synthetic forms of this insecticide have since been developed.

Description: The garden varieties produce large, single, semidouble, or double daisies with pink, red, or white petals and yellow centres on 30 to 60 cm (1 to 2 ft.) stems in June and July. The foliage is dark green and finely divided, almost ferny.

Culture: Painted daisies do well in fertile, moist, well-drained soil in full sun.

Use: They are best planted in diagonal "drifts" in the border so that the yellow, unattractive foliage of late summer can be hidden by adjoining, later-flowering perennials. They are excellent as cut flowers.

Propagation: Propagation is by seed or by division once flowering is complete.

Chrysanthemum coccineum

Alberta Horticultural Association

Chrysanthemum x *superbum*

Ed Toop

Chrysanthemum x *superbum*
'Wirral's Supreme'

Alberta Horticultural Association

Chrysanthemum x *superbum*
Shasta Daisy

History: The common name is derived from Mount Shasta, in California, near which the American plant breeder, Luther Burbank, developed the plant familiar to today's gardeners.

Description: One of the most familiar of all perennials, Shasta daisies produce 5 to 8 cm (2 to 3 in.) white flowers with yellow centres on 60 to 90 cm (2 to 3 ft.) stems in July. The newer, double cultivars are generally not hardy in prairie gardens. 'Alaska', with single flowers, is one of the better cultivars. The dwarf cultivars, such as 'Miss Muffet' or 'Silver Princess' [semi-double, 30 cm (12 in.) in height] seem to hold promise for cold hardiness but need further testing under prairie conditions.

Culture: Shasta daisies do well in full sun or in partial shade in well-drained, evenly moist soil. Like many other perennials, they bloom better when regularly divided, watered, and fertilized.

Use: They provide a foil for contrasting pinks, oranges, and reds in the border, are excellent as cut flowers, and are often utilized in the "night "or "white" garden.

Note: if grown in large masses the rather unpleasant odor of the flowers can become overwhelming.

Propagation: Shasta daisies are easily raised from seed. Larger clumps may be divided every 2 or 3 years.

Chrysanthemum morifolium
Chrysanthemum

Description: The garden chrysanthemums are daisy-like perennials with aromatic, lobed leaves which bloom in late summer and early fall when many other flowers in the border are finished. Those varieties available from seed and most varieties offered by eastern or southern nurseries (or available boxed from chain stores) more often than not flower too late to be of use in prairie gardens.

But prairie gardeners can take heart. Many "early" (late August and September) flowering cultivars have been developed by plant breeders in Western Canada. Among these are 'Morden Cameo', 60 cm (2 ft), double, white; 'Morden Canary', 50 cm (2 ft.), double, yellow; 'Morden Eldorado', 40 cm (16 in.) , double, yellow; 'Morden Gaity', 50 cm (20 in.) double, orange bronze; 'Morden Candy', 50 cm (20 in.), double, pink; 'Morden Delight', 60 cm (2 ft.), double, bronze red; 'Morden Garnet', 50 cm (20 in.), double, red; 'Morden Everest', 40 cm (16 in.), double, white; 'Susan Brandon', 60 cm (2 ft.), semidouble, lavender; and 'Morden Fiesta', 40 cm (16 in.), double, purple. Morden cultivars which are good mound formers are 'Morden Canary', 'Morden Eldorado', 'Morden Everest', and 'Morden Gaiety'.

Culture: Hardy mums need regular division. The best plants are grown from single basal shoot pieces carefully removed from the mother plants in early May. The older woody portions are discarded. By early June they will have developed fibrous roots and be ready for planting out. Care must be taken that the soil is kept evenly moist and that the young shoots are not allowed to dry up under the influence of spring winds.

Plant the "stolons" (young basal shoots) firmly and a little deeper than when they were attached to the mother plant. Mulch well to conserve moisture, reduce soil temperature, and prevent weed seed germination. Because mums are not long-lived, regular dividing and replanting are necessary. Do not remove or clean up dead foliage in the fall if it appears free of disease. Leave it to "catch the snow" and provide extra insulation during the winter and add additional moisture in the spring.

In winters with little snow cover or fluctuating temperatures, even the Morden cultivars must be considered only marginally hardy.

Use: In spite of their high maintenance, chrysanthemums are excellent additions to the border in late summer and early fall and are outstanding as cut flowers.

Propagation: Although these cultivars do not come true from seed, they are easily propagated by division and cuttings and should be available from local nurseries.

Chrysanthemum 'Morden Canary'

Chrysanthemum 'Morden Fiesta'

Chrysanthemum 'Morden Cameo'

Cimicifuga racemosa

Cimicifuga racemosa
Black Snakeroot or Bugbane

Description: An erect plant of 120 to 180 cm (4 to 6 ft.), bugbane bears long racemes of white flowers in July and August. The compound leaves are a dark bronzy green and deeply lobed. Both the common name, "bugbane", and the genus, "Cimicifuga", refer to its reputed insecticidal properties. "Cimex" is Latin for insect while "fugare" means "to flee".

Culture: A native woodland plant, bugbane needs a rich, evenly-moist, organic soil to do well in prairie gardens. It will grow well in sun or partial shade.

Use: It is best used toward the back of a large perennial border, as a specimen plant or naturalized in a woodland setting.

Propagation: Propagation is easiest by division in the spring. Seeds should be sown as soon as they are ripe.

Clematis spp.

Introduction: Besides the better known vining types, there are a few species of herbaceous clematis which are hardy in prairie gardens.

Clematis integrifolia

Clematis integrifolia
Solitary Clematis

Description: The solitary clematis produces blue, nodding, bell-shaped flowers with white centres on 60 to 90 cm (2 to 3 ft.) stems in June and July. The silky seed heads which follow the flowers are also attractive. Although upright in spring, by mid-summer it is somewhat sprawly and the more fastidious gardener might want to provide it with some support.

Culture: Like the climbers, this one does best under evenly moist conditions with a cool root system in a loam soil. Mulching is therefore beneficial. Plant in full sun or partial shade.

Use: It makes a rather unique and attractive addition to the perennial border.

Propagation: Propagation is by division or internodal cuttings (where the basal cut is **not** through the node) taken in spring.

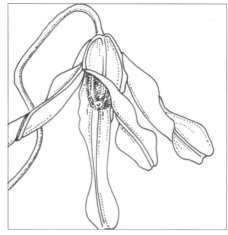

Clematis integrifolia

Clematis recta
Ground Clematis

Description: Another herbaceous perennial, the ground clematis will reach a height of 1 to 1.6 m (3 to 5 ft.), producing fragrant white flowers in June and July. Not a true climber, it tends to sprawl and will be more attractive if given some support over which it is allowed to drape.

Culture: It does well in ordinary soil in full sun.

Use: Too sprawly for a formal border, the ground clematis is useful in a wild garden, planted near a patio to take advantage of its fragrance, or as part of a "white" or "night" garden.

Propagation: Propagation is by division or cuttings. It also tends to self-seed.

Clematis recta

Clematis recta

Convallaria majalis

Convallaria majalis

Convallaria majalis
Lily-of-the-Valley

Description: Lily-of-the-valley, a plant that normally grows to a height of 20 cm (8 in.), produces racemes of fragrant nodding white bells in May or June above wide green leaves.

Note: All plant parts are considered poisonous as is water in which the cut flowers have been placed.

Culture: It does well in partial shade to full shade in evenly moist, organic soil. Plants should be divided and replanted every 3 or 4 years to prevent over crowding (which results in smaller flowers which are fewer in number).

Use: Lily-of-the-valley is an excellent ground cover under trees or other difficult areas. The flowers are often used in arrangements. Because of its aggressive nature, it should not be placed in the border or rock garden.

Propagation: Propagation is by division of the "pips" or small shoots which grow from the rhizomes. This should be done in spring.

Corydalis nobilis

Corydalis nobilis
Siberian Corydalis

Description: A native of Siberia and one of the earliest flowering perennials, corydalis produces heads of yellow flowers which are darker on the petal margins, above fern-like, deeply dissected leaves in May. It is 25 to 30 cm (10 to 12 in.) in height and dies down soon after flowering.

Culture: Plant in full sun or partial shade in well-drained soil. They are fairly drought-tolerant once established.

PERENNIALS FOR THE PLAINS AND PRAIRIES

Use: Corydalis will naturalize readily through self-seeding in partially shaded areas and would do well in an underplanting in a wild garden as well as a rock garden.

Propagation: Established plants do not transplant or divide easily but they do self-sow and young seedlings are easily moved. Collected seeds should be sown as soon as ripe.

Delphinium elatum
Delphinium

Description: An old fashioned garden plant well adapted to prairie conditions, delphiniums bloom in late June and July. The Pacific giant hybrids are the type most commonly seen in prairie gardens. They are 120 to 180 cm (4 to 6 ft.) high with attractive palmate leaves. Mostly double, individual cultivars include 'Black Knight' (deep midnight violet), 'Galahad' (huge clear white), 'Blue bird' (medium blue, white bee), 'Blue Jay' (brilliant blue, dark bee), and 'Guinevere' (light pinkish lavender).

Dwarf cultivars, mainly hybrids of the Chinese delphiniums, are more suitable to the smaller garden, or windier locations, and tend to have a longer blooming period and more finely divided delicate foliage. 'Connecticut Yankee' has single flowers available in blue, white, lavender, and purple and is 45 cm (1.5 ft.) high. 'Blue Fountains' is 75 to 90 cm (2.5 to 3 ft.) high with large double flowers in shades of blue, mauve, purple, and white. *Delphinium cardinale* is not hardy. *Delphinium zalil* is only marginally so, and not long-lived.

Culture: Delphiniums are "heavy feeders" and will benefit from the incorporation of a high phosphorus fertilizer such as bone meal or 11-48-0 in early spring. Taller types should be staked and planted in a sheltered location to prevent wind damage.

All delphiniums need a rich, evenly moist soil which is well-drained and in full sun. Set the plants 60 to 90 cm (2 to 3 ft.) apart in groups of 3 to 5 plants. In the spring, leave about 7 shoots on older plants (any additional shoots may be used as cuttings to produce new plants).

Delphinium elatum 'Galahad'

Delphinium elatum 'Guinevere'

Delphinium 'Connecticut Yankee'

Anita Schill

When delphiniums begin new growth in spring they are often damaged by green larvae (appropriately called "delphinium worms") which feed on new shoots. They should be hand-picked or dusted.

Use: The taller types of delphiniums are best used toward the back of the border and are excellent as cut flowers. The dwarf types are better placed in the middle of the border.

Propagation: Delphiniums may be propagated by seed (expect some variation), softwood cuttings taken when the shoots are about 10 cm (4 in.) high in the spring, or by division, also in early spring. Seed should be frozen for a minimum of 48 hours prior to sowing to break dormancy. Germination is optimum at 13 to 16°C (55 to 60 °F).

Dianthus barbatus

Alberta Horticultural Association

Dianthus barbatus
Sweet William

Description: A biennial or short-lived perennial, sweet William is an old-fashioned garden favorite which has graced English gardens since the time of Shakespeare. Its flowers are fragrant and produced in dense clusters in various shades of white, pink, rose and red throughout its second growing season. Many cultivars are available, ranging in height from 15 to 60 cm (6 to 24 in.).

Culture: They do well in full sun and moist but well-drained soil.

Use: Sweet Williams are excellent in the border, the cottage garden, and as cut flowers.

Propagation: Propagation is by seed.

Dianthus deltoides
Maiden Pinks

Description: Maiden pinks form large mats 8 to 15 cm (3 to 6 in.) in height of dark green foliage which is covered with masses of bright carmine-red or white flowers in June and July.

Culture: Fairly drought tolerant, they demand full sun and well-drained soil. After flowering, shear the flower stems to make the foliage more attractive. Older plants tend to die out in the middle and may need division and replanting of the more vigorous sections from the outer edge from time to time.

Use: Maiden pinks are excellent as a groundcover, in the rock garden, among paving stones or patio blocks, or toward the front of the border.

Propagation: Propagation is easiest by seed. They will also self-sow. Division in early spring is also recommended.

Dianthus deltoides

Dianthus deltoides

Dianthus plumarius
Grass Pinks

Description: Attractive plants of 30 cm (12 in.), with grassy, blue-grey foliage, grass pinks produce a myriad of fragrant carnation-like flowers in June. The flowers are single or double, often fringed, and are available in variations of pink and white. At trials in central Canada in the 1960s, *D. plumarius* was rated medium hardy or surviving "most of the time."

Dianthus allwoodii and *D. alpinus* are both dwarf species [15 cm (6 in.)] which were rated hardy in the Canadian trials.

Dianthus plumarius

Dianthus plumarius

Brian Porter

Culture: Plant in a sunny location in well-drained soil. They will benefit from snow cover to protect them from drying winter and spring winds.

Use: Because of their stature, they are ideal for the rockery or the front of the perennial border. They are fragrant and excellent for cutting.

Propagation: Pinks are easily raised from seed which should be thinly sown. They may also be propagated by stem cuttings (of "elbows") and layering.

Dicentra eximia

Ed Toop

Dicentra eximia
Plume Bleeding Heart

Description: This is a dwarf species with attractive, blue-grey, finely divided foliage forming a rounded plant 30 to 38 cm (12 to 15 in.) high. The flowers are pink, heart-shaped, and bloom in June and then intermittently all summer. It is superior to the common bleeding heart in both its foliage (which does not die down in mid-summer and is generally more attractive) and its long period of bloom.

Dicentra formosa (western or Pacific bleeding heart) is similar but with deeper pink flowers. Both are native to North America. The cultivar 'Luxuriant' is thought to be a hybrid of *Dicentra eximia* and *Dicentra formosa*. It is about 38 cm (15 in.) tall with deep pink flowers and attractive foliage.

Culture: Plant in partial shade with even moisture.

Use: It is best utilized in the shaded garden, the wild garden, and because of its dwarf stature, in moist, shaded areas of a rock garden.

Propagation: Propagation is by division in early spring, by seed, and stem or root cuttings. It also tends to self-seed.

Dicentra spectabilis
Common Bleeding Heart

Description: The common bleeding heart was first introduced to Britain from Japan in 1847.

It has graceful, arching branches to 90 cm (3 ft.) with attractive finely divided foliage and pink, heart-shaped flowers in May and June. 'Alba' is a pure white form.

Culture: Bleeding hearts do well in partial shade with even moisture and can remain in the same location for years. The foliage tends to die back after blooming so it is a good idea to plant other, later-blooming perennials in front of them.

Use: They do well in a shady border or a wild garden and are useful as cut flowers.

Propagation: Propagation is by seed which is sown in fall to germinate the following spring, or can be stratified for 6 weeks at refrigerator temperatures prior to sowing. Bleeding heart may also be increased by root cuttings or division in early spring.

Dicentra spectabilis

Dicentra spectabilis

Dictamnus albus (D. fraxinella)
Gasplant or Dittany

Description: One of the more attractive but rarely seen perennials, the gasplant is extremely hardy and long-lived. It has dark green, glossy, compound leaves. Racemes of white or pink flowers are produced on 90 cm (3 ft.) stems in June. The entire plant exudes a pungent, lemon-like fragrance when handled from whence the common name is derived. If a lighted match is held under the flower or seed clusters they will give off a flash of light. The volatile oils contained within the plant may cause skin inflammation or blistering. Ingesting of plant parts can be fatal.

Culture: Gasplants do best in a loamy soil in full sun. They should be left undisturbed and can live for 20 years or more. Once established, they are fairly drought-tolerant.

Dictamnus albus

Dictamnus albus

Use: They are excellent as a specimen plant or in the perennial border.

Propagation: Sow fresh but ripened seed outdoors in late August or September. Seeds should germinate the following spring. Division is not recommended as the plant should not be disturbed.

Digitalis purpurea

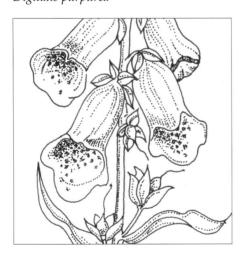
Digitalis grandiflora

Digitalis spp.
Foxglove

Description: Under sheltered conditions in the wooded areas or with consistent snow cover, *Digitalis grandiflora* (yellow foxglove) is considered likely to survive. *D. purpurea* (common foxglove) is not considered hardy in the northern prairie regions. The yellow foxglove bears spikes of tubular flowers in July on 60 cm (2 ft.) plants. As the Latin name "digitalis" suggests, foxgloves are a source of extremely poisonous cardiac glycosides that affect the heart. Though widely used for medicinal purposes the whole plant is poisonous and should not be ingested.

Culture: Foxgloves do well in well-drained organic soils with even moisture in partial shade.

Use: They are excellent in the partially shaded border or naturalized in a wooded or shaded garden and are ideal as cut flowers.

Propagation: They are easily propagated form seed or by division in early spring.

Doronicum caucasicum (D. cordatum)
Leopardsbane

Description: Mound-shaped plants produce yellow, daisy-like flowers 5 cm (2 in.) in diameter in early June on 45 cm (18 in.) stems. The leaves are kidney or heart-shaped and attractive.

Culture: Grow leopardsbane in an organic, evenly moist soil in partial shade. Mulching to ensure a cool root system is beneficial. Because the foliage often dies down after flowering is complete, it is advisable to plant *Doronicum* next to later flowering perennials which will fill the vacant space.

Use: They are best planted in diagonal "drifts" in a shaded border and are excellent as cut flowers.

Propagation: Propagation is by seed or by division soon after flowering.

Doronicum caucasicum

Draba aizoon (D. lasiocarpa)
Aizoon

Description: A tufted, alpine plant with diminutive leaves forming tight rosettes, *Draba* is one of the first perennials to bloom in the spring with tiny yellow flowers on 5 cm (2 in.) stems.

Culture: It is best grown in full sun in a well-drained, gritty soil into which peat moss has been incorporated.

Use: *Draba* is an excellent plant for the rock garden.

Propagation: Propagation is easiest by division or seed.

Draba aizoon

Dracocephalum grandiflorum
Dragonhead

Dracocephalum grandiflorum

Description: A member of the mint family, characterized by square stems and opposite leaves, the dragonhead produces hooded, two-lipped, deep blue flowers about 20 cm (8 in.) in height in late May and early June. A native of Siberia, it is reliably hardy in the prairie environment. The species *Dracocephalum sibiricum* is also a good hardy plant and slightly taller than *Dracocephalum grandiflorum*.

Culture: Plant in well-drained soil in full sun or partial shade.

Use: Dragonheads are best utilized in the rock garden or massed toward the front of the border.

Propagation: Propagation is easiest by division.

Dryas octopetala
Mountain Avens

Dryas octopetala

Description: Actually a **subshrub**, *Dryas* is a member of the rose family with a creeping habit and evergreen, oak-like leaves. It produces white flowers, 25 to 50 mm (1 to 2 in.) in diameter, in May and June.

Culture: It flourishes in sunny, well-drained situations.

Use: Mountain avens makes an interesting and unusual rock garden plant.

Propagation: Propagation is by seed or cuttings taken in summer.

Duchesnea indica
Mock-Strawberry

Description: A native of Korea, this diminutive but aggressive plant has become naturalized over much of North America. Only 25 mm (1 in.) in height, it resembles a strawberry in its flowers (which are yellow rather than white), foliage, and fruit but the latter are not considered edible. The stolons increase rapidly and may need some control. It has been reported as tender in some areas and is best planted in a sheltered location with adequate snow cover.

Culture: It grows well in full sun or shade on well-drained soil.

Use: The mock-strawberry is best utilized as a groundcover in open areas or on slopes. It should not be placed in a border or in a rock garden because of its competitive nature.

Propagation: Propagation is by runners.

Duchesnea indica

Echinops ritro (E. exaltatus)
Small Globe Thistle

Description: Characterized by spines on the flowers, leaves and stems, the globe thistle is 90 to 120 cm (3 to 4 ft.) in height with steel blue flowers the size of golf balls in late summer. Because of its prickly nature it it not an easy plant to weed around or to handle. "Echinops" is from the Greek word for hedgehog and aptly describes the plant's spiny nature. The undersides of the leaves are silvery white in appearance.

Culture: It thrives in well-drained soil in full sun and is quite drought-tolerant.

Use: Globe thistle makes a striking specimen plant for the back of a large perennial border and is often used in dried arrangements. For good color retention they are best cut as soon as the flower begins to open.

Echinops ritro

Hugh Knowles

Echinops ritro

Propagation: Propagation is by division, root cuttings or by seed. Plants will self seed to a limited extent and sometimes die after flowering. Seedlings will be variable in quality.

Erigeron

Erigeron

Erigeron speciosus
Oregon Fleabane

Description: These aster-like perennials have pink, mauve, blue and purple flowers with yellow centers and bloom in mid-summer. They are 30 to 60 cm (1 to 2 ft.) in height. The dried flowers were once placed near beds in the belief that they would drive away fleas, hence the common name, "fleabane." Of those tested in central Canada, the Oregon fleabane with its small blue flowers has proved the most reliable. 'Merstham Glory' has mauve flowers while 'Quakeress' has pink flowers. Both are cultivars of the Oregon fleabane.

Culture: Fleabanes do well in full soil and ordinary, well-drained garden soil.

Use: Excellent as cut flowers, they are also useful grouped in the mid-height range of the sunny perennial border where they will flower for up to a month. Partial shade will prolong bloom. Newer cultivars will need further testing in the prairie region but many should prove hardy.

Propagation: They can be grown from seed, cuttings or division.

Eryngium spp.
Sea Holly

Description: Somewhat resembling ornamental thistles, sea hollies have blue to grey flowers above deeply cut, shiny foliage. The flowers look like a cone flower with a silvery ruft-like bract at its base. Like thistles, they are prickly!

Species which have proven hardy include *E. amethystinum*, the amethyst sea holly, which is 45 cm (18 in.) high with steel grey leaves and blue flowers, *E. alpinum*, the alpine sea holly, which is 60 to 90 cm (2 to 3 ft.) in height and has larger flowers, and *E. planum*, which is 90 cm (3 ft.) with blue flowers. *Eryngium alpinum* is more tolerant of shade and clay soils. *Eryngium planum* is much more invasive than the other species. All begin blooming in mid-summer and hold their flowers until fall.

Culture: Sea hollies do well in full sun in well-drained situations and are tolerant of both poor soils and drought.

Use: They are used for both fresh and dried arrangements and fit in well in a sunny perennial border. For the best color retention in dried arrangements, the flowers should be picked when fully open.

Propagation: They are easily grown from seed as well as cuttings (which are best taken in early spring). Seed should be sown as soon as it is ripe in late summer. It will germinate the following spring. Because of their thick tap root, sea hollies should be disturbed as little as possible once established.

Eryngium planum

Eryngium alpinum

Erysimum asperum (Cherianthus allioni)
Siberian Wallflower

Description: Actually a biennial, the Siberian wallflower germinates and produces vegetative leafy growth during its first growing season and flowers, sets seed, and dies the following growing season. The seed produced will germinate during the second growing season so a pattern of continual flowering is achieved although each individual plant will only live for two years. The bright orange flowers appear on stems about 38 cm (15 in.) in height in June and July. The flowers are fragrant.

Erysimum

Erysimum

Saskatchewan Department of Agriculture & Food

Culture: They do well in sunny or partially shaded locations in well drained soils.

Use: Wallflowers are easily naturalized in drifts in both the perennial border and rock garden.

Propagation: Siberian wallflowers are easily raised from seed.

Euphorbia cyparissias

Gail Rankin

Euphorbia epithymoides

Alberta Horticultural Association

Euphorbia cyparissias
Cypress Spurge

Description: Although native to Europe, cypress spurge has escaped from cultivation in the eastern United States. It has a deceptively delicate appearance with fine linear leaves and tiny, greenish-yellow bracts in late May and early June. Height is about 30 cm (12 in.). Like other members of the spurge family, its stems will exude a milky sap when broken which may irritate the skin.

A close relative, cushion spurge (*Euphorbia epithymoides*) is less hardy and unless sheltered may not be reliable.

Culture: Cypress spurge does well in full sun with good drainage on poor soils.

Use: It is excellent as a drought-resistant groundcover, spreading by underground stolons. It is not recommended that it be planted in association with more valuable or less vigorous plants because of its competitive ability. Some gardeners in milder areas of the prairie region regard this perennial as a "weed" to be avoided. It is considered a noxious weed in some areas.

Propagation: Propagation is by division. It may also be grown from seeds or cuttings.

PERENNIALS FOR THE PLAINS AND PRAIRIES

Festuca ovina **var.** *glauca*
Sheep's Fescue

Festuca ovina var. *glauca*

Description: An attractive blue-grey ornamental grass, sheep's fescue is about 25 cm (10 in.) high with fine wiry blades growing in tufted clumps. It is one of the few reliably hardy ornamental grasses available to prairie gardeners. 'Skinner's Blue' is valued for the contrasting golden seed heads.

Culture: Sheep's fescue will grow in full sun or partial shade with good drainage and is quite drought tolerant once established. The foliage color will be less blue in shaded areas. There seems to be some variability in hardiness among seedlings.

Use: It is useful as an accent plant in a rock garden or for edging a more formal perennial border. It is totally non-invasive.

Propagation: Propagation is by division or seed.

Filipendula **spp.**
Meadowsweet

Filipendula ulmaria 'Flore-pleno'

Description: Resembling spireas, the meadowsweets are handsome plants, 1 to 2 m (3 to 6 ft.) in height, with deeply cut compound leaves. The dainty plumes of white or pink flowers are composed of masses of tiny florets. They are an excellent substitute in those areas where astilbes do poorly.

Recommended species include queen-of-the-prairie (*F. rubra*), 120 to 180 cm (4 to 6 ft.) in height with peach-pink flowers in June; queen-of-the-meadow (*F. ulmaria*) which is 60 to 90 cm (2 to 3 ft.) with creamy white flowers and can be used to produce a greenish-yellow dye, and dropwort meadowsweet (*F. vulgaris*, formerly *F. hexapetala*) which is 30 cm (12 in.) with panicles of creamy white flowers in July with carrot-like dark green foliage.

Filipendula ulmaria

Culture: Meadowsweets thrive in shady situations with even moisture and soils enriched with peat moss or other organic matter. Spider mites may be a problem during periods of hot dry weather.

Use: They do well in the shady border or naturalized near ponds or in woodland situations. They are useful as cut flowers.

Propagation: Propagation is by seed and division.

Gaillardia aristata

Gaillardia aristata 'Goblin'

Gaillardia aristata
Blanket Flower

Description: Blooming from mid-summer until hard frost, the blanket flower produces 5 cm (2 in.) daisies in shades of maroon, red, orange, and yellow on 60 to 90 cm (2 to 3 ft.) stems. 'Goblin' is a compact cultivar of 30 to 45 cm (12 to 18 in.) which is ideal for the front of the border or rock garden. Because they are later emerging in the spring than other perennials, it is a good idea to label them so as not to accidently dig them up.

Some of the newer cultivars are actually hybrids between the annual and perennial species and do not tend to be as long lived as might be desired. Those listed as *Gaillardia* x *grandiflora* are crosses between the perennial *G. artistata* and *G. pulchella* which is an annual. Among these newer cultivars are 'Burgundy', 'Dazzler', 'Goblin', and the 'Monarch' strain.

Culture: Blanket flowers do well in full sun with good drainage. They are drought tolerant and will thrive in poorer soils.

Use: They are excellent as cut flowers and in the border.

Propagation: Gaillardias are easily grown from seed and will self-seed to a limited extent. Volunteer seedlings are easily transplanted to newer locations. They may also be increased by division or root cuttings. Root cuttings should be 25 mm (1 in.) long and taken in the fall, laid in flats and covered with 15 mm (0.5 in.) of sand. Place them in a cool, light greenhouse where they will form plants by spring.

Gaillardia aristata

Gentiana spp.
Gentian

Description: As the name implies, gentians are noted for their true blue flowers. The Andrews or bottle gentian (*G. andrewsii*) is native to the woodlands of the northeastern United States and Canada. The species was named after Henry C. Andrews, an English botanical artist and engraver, who published important botanical works early in the nineteenth century. It has shiny, dark green leaves and violet blue flowers on 30 to 38 cm (12 to 15 in.) stems in July. It is sometime called the closed gentian because its flowers never open fully but seem to remain in bud-like form. The flowers are borne in clusters in the axils of the upper leaves which are **sessile**.

Native to Iran and Turkestan, the seven-lobed gentian (*G. septemfida*) is 15 to 23 cm (6 to 9 in.) high with clusters of clear blue, open, bell or trumpet-shaped flowers. The stem spreads along the ground for several centimetres terminating in a flower cluster in July. *G. acaulis* is native to the Swiss Alps and is reported to be hardy. Only 10 cm (4 in.) tall it blooms in May or June. There are also late summer and fall flowering gentians. Two Asian species to be recommended are *G. sarreri* and *G. sino-ornate* as well as their hybrid *G x macaulayi*. Two good cultivars are 'Susan Jane' and 'Inverleith'.

Culture: Gentians grow best under evenly moist, shaded conditions in acidic, organic soils.

Use: They are best utilized in a woodland or natural garden. The bottle gentian does well under bog conditions.

Gentiana septemfida

Gentiana

Gentiana acaulis

Propagation: Propagation is by seed which is either given a cold treatment of several months or else sown outdoors in the fall to germinate the following spring. However, germination may not take place until the second spring (in which case moisture may have been the critical factor). Gentian will sometimes self-seed. They may also be divided.

Geranium sanguineum

Geranium nodosum

Geranium spp.
Cranesbill Geranium

History: Geraniums were mentioned in herbals as early as the 16th century and were said to heal afflictions of the kidneys, genitals, lungs, and eyes!

Description: The perennial geraniums or cranesbills form a group of over 400 species, the majority of which are found in the Northern hemisphere. (These are not to be confused with the houseplant or bedding plants which are actually *Pelargoniums*.) The name "geranium" comes from the Greek word "geranos" which means "crane" and refers to the beak-like shape of the seed pod.

The large number of species and cultivars combined with a lack of methodical hardiness trials as well as the presence of either unnamed or misnamed plants has led to confusion as to which species are indeed hardy in the prairie region. Until correctly labeled plants have been over-wintered for successive years it is difficult to make recommendations.

One may have half a dozen different perennial geraniums in a border which are indeed hardy but not have a clue as to which ones they are as they found their way into the garden simply labeled "cranesbill."

Four species were rated as "hardy" in trials in central Canada, in the early 1960s.

Geranium grandiflorum (also referred to as *Geranium himalayense*) or the lilac cranesbill is 30 to 45 cm (12 to 15 in.) in height, bushy, and has large 5 cm (2 in.) diameter blue flowers with red or purple veins. The leaves have 5 to 7 lobes. There is also a double-flowered selection usually listed as *G. grandiflorum* 'Plenum'.

Geranium ibericum (the Caucasian cranesbill) is 45 to 50 cm (18 to 20 in.) with violet blue flowers with feathered purple veins and leaves with 5 to 7 lobes. 'Album' is 60 cm (2 ft.) with white flowers. 'Johnson's Blue' is 45 cm (18 in.) with bright blue flowers.

Geranium ibericum var. *platypetalum* (also referred to as *Geranium playpetalum*), the flatpetal cranesbill, is 60 cm (2 ft.) and has deep violet flowers with reddish veins. Its leaves are larger and 5 lobed.

Geranium macrorrhizum, the big root geranium, has many natural hybrids and cultivars. It is 30 to 38 cm (12 to 15 in.) high with pink flowers and 5-lobed leaves. It makes an excellent ground cover because the leaves are held horizontally and therefore shade and discourage weed growth underneath. The leaves are fragrant and are the source of commercial oil of geranium. Two cultivars are 'Ingwersen's Variety' with pink flowers held in sprays above the leaves and 'Album' which is white.

All of the cranesbills have attractive foliage and bloom in June and July. But figuring out which you have may be confusing!

Geranium sanguineum and *G. nodosum* have also been successfully grown in some prairie gardens. The former is 30 cm (12 in.) tall with purple to magenta flowers and the latter is similar in height with purple (red-veined) flowers.

Culture: If the nomenclature leaves the gardener baffled there is compensation in knowing that these plants generally require minimal care, have an extended flowering season, and will grow in sun or shade on most soils.

Use: They are wonderful additions to the perennial border, the rock garden and as groundcovers. Although a few types will re-seed, few are invasive.

Propagation: Cranesbill geraniums are easily propagated by seed (first chill the seed for 3 weeks in the refrigerator to break dormancy), division, or stem or root cuttings.

Geranium macrorrhizum

Geranium ibericum

Geum x borisii

Geum

Geum spp.
Geum or Avens

Description: *Geum urbanum* var. *sibiricum* (Siberian avens) has been rated hardy in parts of prairie Canada, whereas the two cultivars of *G. chiloense*, 'Lady Stratheden' and' Mrs. Bradshaw', have not. Siberian avens is 25 to 30 cm (10 in.) high with attractive dark green, compound leaves and brilliant orange-red flowers in May and early June. While fully hardy and long lived, the basal clumps are slow to increase and never invasive.

Geum triflorum (three-flowered avens) is a native plant which adapts well to rock garden conditions. Thirty-centimetre (12 in.) stems arise from basal rosettes to produce 3 nodding pink flowers ("triflorum" means three-flowered.) The seed pods are airy and misty and smoky pink in color which accounts for its other common name, "Prairie Smoke." *Geum* x *borisii* is rated less hardy than the above species and may need protection. It is 25 cm (10 in.) in height with yellow flowers.

Culture: Geums are easily grown in full sun in well-drained soil.

Use: They are useful in both the rock garden and toward the front of a perennial border.

Propagation: Propagation is easiest by division or cuttings taken in early summer. Seed is slow with low germination rates.

Glechoma hederacea

Glechoma hederacea variegata (*Nepeta hederacea*)
Variegated Creeping Charlie

Description: While the species can be weedlike and invasive, the form variegata is less vigorous and noted for its attractive green and yellow foliage. A member of the mint family, it has square stems and leaves which are opposite, rounded and 15 mm (0.5 in.) in diameter. The flowers are blue, in whorled clusters. Its habit of growth is mat-like.

Culture: *Glechoma*, also called ground ivy, does well in sun or shade in ordinary soil.

Use: It can be used as a ground cover, in the rock garden, or at the front of the border.

Propagation: It is easily propagated by division.

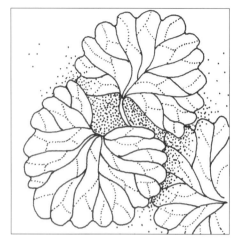

Glechoma hederacea

Gypsophila paniculata
Babysbreath

Description: Well known in prairie gardens, babysbreath is a dainty old-fashioned flower with a misty grace and masses of tiny white flowers on 90 cm (3 ft.) stems from July to freeze-up. Unfortunately in some areas it has escaped from cultivation and naturalized itself in ditches and pasture land where it has proved difficult to eradicate. In some areas it has been declared a noxious weed and nurseries are not allowed to sell it.

The double-flowered form (*G. paniculata* 'Flore Pleno') is available from seed but not all of the seedlings will be double. 'Bristol Fairy' is also double but is sterile and produces no seed. It is generally propagated by tissue culture. In the last decade, many of the types which were once grafted are now being produced by tissue culture. Because they are on their own roots, these tend to be longer lived.

Gypsophila paniculata var. *compacta plena* is only 30 cm (12 in.) with double white flowers. It has been grown successfully in more sheltered locations but needs further testing.

Gypsophila pacifica is similar to *G. paniculata* but is less florific, has pink flowers, and is more spreading in habit.

Culture: Babysbreath does well in hot dry locations in full sun on well-drained soils. The name "Gypsophila" means gypsum-loving and indicates its preference for limestone soils, of which the prairie grasslands have plenty. Because of their deep tap root they are extremely drought tolerant once established. (This same tap root makes them difficult to transplant except when fairly young.) They may need staking in windy or exposed sites.

Gail Rankin

Gypsophila paniculata 'Flore Pleno'

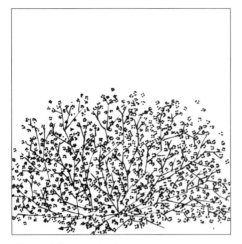

Gypsophila paniculata

Use: Babysbreath are excellent as cut flowers and in dried arrangements as well as in the border itself. They are also useful for planting behind spring bulbs or Oriental poppies where their sheer mass can fill in the spaces left vacant in late summer.

Propagation: Propagation is by seed and cuttings.

Gypsophila repens 'Rosea'

Olds College Collection

Gypsophila repens
Creeping Babysbreath

Description: Originally from the Alps and Pyrenees Mountains, trailing or creeping babysbreath is a prostrate plant of 15 cm (6 in.) with small leaves and tiny white flowers in mid-summer. *Gypsophila repens* 'Rosea' has pink flowers. 'Rosyveil' (also known as 'Rosenschlier') is a hybrid of 'Rosea' and *G. paniculata*, 45 cm (18 in.) high with semi-double to double pinkish to white flowers.

Culture: Like the taller forms, they do well in full sun and well-drained soil.

Use: They are ideal for the rock garden or toward the front of the perennial border.

Propagation: Propagation is by seed and cuttings. Babysbreath are difficult to move or divide due to their tap root.

Gypsophila 'Rosenschlier'

Brian Porter

PERENNIALS FOR THE PLAINS AND PRAIRIES

Heliopsis helianthoides
Rough Heliopsis

Description: A native of North America, rough heliopsis produces large yellow daisies resembling small sun flowers on 90 cm (3 ft.) stems in July and August. The word "rough" refers to the sandpaper quality of the leaves. Cultivars which have proven hardy include 'Excelsa' with nearly double, chrome yellow flowers, 'Incomparabilis' with rich golden yellow, double flowers 8 cm (3 in.) in diameter, and 'Light of Lodden' with bright yellow blooms.

Culture: Heliopsis do best in an open, sunny location in any fertile soil with even moisture. In hotter, drier parts of the prairies afternoon shade is beneficial.

Use: They are well suited toward the back of the perennial border and are long-lasting both on the plant and as a cut flower.

Propagation: Propagation is by seed, cuttings, and division of rootstock.

Heliopsis helianthoides 'Incomparabilis'

Heliopsis helianthoides

Hemerocallis spp.
Daylily

Description: Not true lilies, daylilies are so named because each flower lasts only 24 hours, but an individual plant, once established, will continue to bloom for several weeks with 50 to 100 or more buds. The flowers do not necessarily close up at night but may remain luminous in the moonlight. Heights vary from dwarf cultivars of 45 cm (18 in.) to those of 120 cm (4 ft.). Colors range from shades of yellow through to orange, pink, red, and mahogany. The form of the flowers themselves may be open or recurved with petals which are strap-shaped to those which are saucer-like. The grass-like foliage remains attractive throughout the growing season.

Like iris, hosta, and peonies, there are hundreds of daylily cultivars. Except for some of the newer hybrids, most will be reliably hardy. Among the recommended species and

Hemerocallis sp.

Hemerocallis sp.

Ed Toop

Hemerocallis sp.

cultivars are *Hemerocallis flava*, *H. gracilis*, 'Stella D'Oro', 'Anna Warner', 'Copper Summer', 'Derby Bound', 'Geraldine Dean',' Pastoral Symphony', 'Purple Quest', 'Scotland', 'Trident', 'Three Tiers' and 'Yellow Pinwheel'.

Culture: Daylilies are one of the most adaptable, low-maintenance, and insect and disease-free perennials available. They will grow equally well in sun or shade (although flowering may be somewhat reduced) and although they do best with adequate moisture, they are quite drought tolerant.

Use: Daylilies are excellent in the perennial border, naturalized in moist areas, or massed as ground cover. An added bonus is their edibility! The tubers can be sautéed or fried, and the buds and flowers can be sautéed or used as a garnish in meat dishes or salads.

Propagation: Although daylilies can be raised from seed, the easiest method of propagation is division. Cultivars will not come true from seed and should be propagated by division. The roots are fleshy, and given adequate after-care, can be planted, transplanted, or divided at almost anytime, although this is best done in spring. Each clump will eventually have a spread of 75 to 90 cm (2.5 to 3 ft.), so make allowance for future growth when spacing them.

Heuchera 'Brandon Pink'

Gabe Botar

Heuchera spp.
Coral Bells or Alumroot

Description: Coral bells is one of the most satisfactory of perennials. It is long blooming, insect and disease resistant, wind tolerant, drought tolerant, and pleasing throughout the growing season. Non-invasive and long-lived, the clumps will remain tidy, increasing gradually in size.

Although the species *Heuchera sanguinea* proved of only medium hardiness at trials in central Canada, several hybrids developed out of breeding programs there have proven hardy on the Canadian prairies. 'Brandon Pink', 'Brandon Glow' and' Northern Fire' are all about 50 to 60 cm (20 to 24 in.) with rosettes of dark green scalloped leaves. They have a long period of bloom with stalks of dainty bells held on wiry stems.' Northern Fire' is dark red while 'Brandon Pink' is a deep pink and 'Brandon Glow' a darker pink with foliage mottled with white. 'Brandon Glow' is slightly shorter than the others.

These were derived from crosses of *H. richardsonii*, a species native to the drier parts of the North American plains with yellow-green flowers, and *H. sanguinea* which has the red flowers but lacks hardiness.

The roots are rich in tannin and very astringent, hence one of the common names, "alum root."

Culture: They should be planted in full sun in well-drained soil. They may not do as well in heavier (clay) soils. Although they are drought tolerant, consistent regular watering will extend the period of bloom.

Use: Coral bells are ideal for the rockery, the front of the perennial border, massed as a ground cover, or as grave side plantings where their demand for maintenance is minimal. They are also useful as cut flowers.

Propagation: Propagation of these hybrids is by division, after flowering, or in spring. Most varieties available from seed are not reliably hardy.

Heuchera

Heuchera

Hosta **spp.**
Plantain Lily or Funkia

Description: Grown mainly for their foliage, hosta vary in height from 15 cm to 122 cm (6 to 40 in.). The leaves may be heart-shaped or strapped, in shades of green, blue, or variegated with white, cream, or gold. The leaf texture itself may be smooth, grooved, or ribbed, flat, wavy or even have a sear-sucker appearance. The trumpet-shaped flowers are white, pink, mauve, or blue with a few types being fragrant. They are low-maintenance, non-invasive plants which form slowly-increasing clumps and seldom need division.

There are hundreds of species and cultivars of *Hosta* available and much confusion in the naming or nomenclature. Among those recommended are: *H. caerulea* (*H. ventricosa*), *H. fortunei*, *H. fortunei* 'Aureo-marginata',

Hosta fortunei

Hosta sieboldiana

Hosta undulata

H. undulata (*H. undulata variegata*), *H. undulata* 'Albo-marginata', *H. nakaiana*, *H. lancifolia*, *H. sieboldiana*, 'Honeybells', and 'Royal Standard', 'Francee', and 'Golden Tiara'.

Culture: They prefer partial or full shade and an evenly moist, organic soil, and will benefit from a mulch during the heat of summer. Slugs may sometimes be a problem.

Use: Hostas are ideal for shaded portions of the perennial border, massing, woodland gardens, moist areas, or bordering a water garden. Dwarf cultivars may be used for edging while the taller types are useful as accent plants.

Propagation: While they may be grown from seed, plants will take several years to reach an acceptable size. Variegated types may not come true from seed. The most common and easiest method of propagation is by division in spring. Commercially, many are now propagated by tissue culture.

Iberis sempervirens

Iberis sempervirens
Perennial Candytuft

Description: A 30 cm (1 ft.), mounded, evergreen perennial, (sometimes considered more of a dwarf shrub or sub-shrub), candytuft is covered in dense clusters of bright white flowers in early June.

The genus name, "Iberis," is derived from Iberia (Spain) from which many of the species originate. Among the cultivars recommended for prairie gardens are 'Snowflake' and 'Purity'.

Culture: Candytuft does well in full sun and well-drained soil. Because of its evergreen nature, it will benefit from a cover of evergreen boughs in the fall (once the ground has frozen) which will catch the snow and provide some shelter from drying winter winds. In winters with little snowfall, it may suffer from occasional browning with consequently fewer flowers. Once established, plants should not be disturbed. Light shearing after flowering will keep the plant compact, avoid center openings, and reduce seed set.

Use: It is ideally suited to the rock garden or the front of a perennial border. Some cultivars are fragrant. They are excellent as cut flowers in smaller bouquets and arrangements.

Propagation: Candytuft is easily raised from seed but it takes two years to flower. It may also be propagated from stem or root cuttings.

Iberis sempervirens

Inula ensifolia
Swordleaf Inula

Description: Inula has small linear leaves and yellow daisy-like flowers 4 cm (1.5 in.) in diameter, blooming in late July and August. The plants themselves are compact and mound-like, about 30 cm (12 in.) in height.

A similar plant, *Buphthalmum salicifolium*, is often confused with inula, but these have proved to be only marginally hardy at trials in central Canada.

Culture: They do well in full sun or partial shade in well-drained soil with even moisture. Once established they tend to be fairly drought tolerant.

Use: Inula is excellent both as a rockery plant and toward the front of the perennial border.

Propagation: They are easily propagated by division but may also be grown from seed.

Inula ensifolia

Iris x *germanica*

Iris x *germanica* 'Radiant Apogee'

Iris x *germanica*

Iris x *germanica*
Bearded Iris

Description: The original German bearded iris, from which so many of the garden cultivars have been at least in part derived, is a native of central and southern Europe. An old fashioned perennial, cultivated since ancient times and introduced into European gardens centuries ago, it is a grassy plant, characterized by broad, sword-like leaves. The flowers consist of three upright petals, called "standards," and three down-facing ones, called "falls." The fuzzy growth of hairs on the falls is called "the beard." In catalogues, the flowers are usually described in terms of their standards and falls.

The modern bearded iris are complex hybrids with diverse parentage. There is tremendous variability in color, form, and size, as well as hardiness, in the thousands of cultivars now available. Although their blooming period is relatively short, two to three weeks, their show is spectacular, with colors ranging from dark purple to blue, white, yellow, pink, and peach. (The name "iris" is derived from the Greek word for rainbow.) Miniatures begin blooming in early May, followed by standard dwarfs in late May, intermediates in early June, and tall and miniature talls in mid-June. They range in height from 15 to 100 cm (6 to 40 in.).

Iris pumila is one of the species that has been crossed with the taller bearded types to produce the miniature standard dwarf cultivars. *Iris pumila* is itself variable in flower color but is under 15 cm (6 in.) in height with finger-sized foliage. Anything larger is undoubtedly a hybrid.

Prairie gardeners will do best buying iris locally where they have been field tested for hardiness by nurserymen for several seasons. Few of the newer hybrids have been extensively tested in the prairie environment, and hardiness may sometimes be sacrificed in the development of new colors, forms, or larger size. Iris that are short to medium in height are usually better suited to prairie conditions than the taller types.

Culture: Bearded iris hybrids are generally adapted to full sun and good drainage. Root rot is encouraged by shade and soggy soil. If encroaching trees begin to shade iris, they may become less vigorous and less free flowering.

Use: Bearded iris are excellent plants for edging or the foreground to middle ground height range of the perennial border. Their foliage remains attractive throughout the season.

Propagation: Iris can be grown from seed but germination is very slow and irregular with flowering taking up to three years. It is easier to divide older plants every three or four years. The best time to plant and divide bearded iris is in July or early August after they have flowered.

When dividing an older clump, first cut the leaves off 8 cm (3 in.) above the rhizome to form a "fan". Then dig up the entire clump and either shake off all the loose soil or wash it off with a hose. Cut out and discard all decayed roots and shoots. Divide the clump into small sections, each one containing a piece of rhizome with a fan of leaves attached. Pieces from the outer part of the clump are younger and more vigorous and are the best ones for replanting.

When replanting, set the rhizome just below soil level, digging a shallow trench [5 to 8 cm (2 to 3 in.) deep] on either side of it. Place the roots in the trench on either side of the rhizome and cover them with fine soil, firming the soil afterwards. The top of the rhizome should remain exposed or be just covered with soil if winter losses have been a problem. Water well. (Deep planting will not kill the iris but may retard blooming and make them more susceptible to soft rot diseases.) Space the rhizomes 25 to 30 cm (10 to 12 in.) apart. The appearance of the bed is sparse the first year, but they soon fill in.

Some growers recommend mulching around the base of the iris prior to their first winter to even out possible temperature fluctuations and provide a measure of insulation. Once established, this practice is not needed unless cultivars are only marginally hardy.

Among the recommended cultivars are:

Miniature Bearded Iris	Standard Dwarf Bearded Iris	Intermediate Bearded Iris
April Ballet	Banbury Ruffles	Sea Patrol
Zipper	Mister Roberts	Dresden Candleglow
Mama's Pet	Velvet Caper	Maroon Caper
Bright White	White Gem	Early Frost
Pixie Pink	Hazel's Pink	Pink Kitten
Tic Tac	Stitch Witch	Early Edition
	Circlette of Gold	
	Path of Gold	

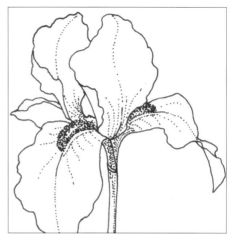

Iris x *germanica*

Iris x *germanica* 'April Ballet'

Iris x *germanica* 'Red Pixie'

Iris pumila

Miniature Tall Bearded Iris	Tall Bearded Iris
Doll Ribbons	Latin Lover
Chichee	Red Baron
New Idea	Stepping Out
Aachen Elf	Toll Gate
Winter Olympics	

Iris pseudacorus

Iris pseudacorus

Iris pseudacorus
Yellowflag Iris

Description: A native of lake sides and other moist areas, the yellowflag iris is 90 cm (3 ft.) in height with green to blue-green foliage and yellow flowers in June.

Culture: In spite of its native habitat it seems to adapt to drier soils, but like most iris demands full sun.

Use: Due to its foliage alone, it is an excellent addition to the border as a bold accent plant. The yellowflag iris is also well adapted to water gardens or waterside plantings.

Propagation: Propagation is easiest by division.

Iris sibirica Hybrids
Siberian Iris

Description: Hybrids of the Siberian and Oriental iris are usually taller [60 to 120 cm (2 to 4 ft.)] than the bearded iris but have narrower leaves and more delicate looking flowers. They bloom in June. Although they appear very fragile, they actually stand up to wind and winter better than the bearded types. Flower colors range from pale blue to purple and white.

Note: The *Iris kaempferi* (Japanese iris) and its hybrids are not generally considered hardy in the prairie climate.

Culture: These Siberian hybrids do best in a deep loamy soil to which organic matter has been added to hold moisture. Place in full or partial sun with even moisture. In hotter, drier regions, afternoon shade is beneficial. They should not be allowed to dry out. They are slower growing than the bearded iris and should not need division for 8 to 10 years. They are best planted in September.

Use: They are excellent massed in the perennial border or in association with ponds or water gardens.

Propagation: Siberian iris are most easily propagated from division in spring but the species may also be grown from seed.

Iris sibirica

Iris sibirica

Lamiastrum galeobdolon var. *variegatum*

Brian Porter

Lamiastrum galeobdolon **var. 'Variegatum'** *(Lamium galeobdolon)*
Deadnettle or Yellow Archangel

Description: A member of the mint family, deadnettle is 30 to 45 cm (12 to 18 in.) high with square stems and opposite leaves. The attractive variegated foliage is dark green with silver. Clusters of yellow flowers are borne in the leaf axils in early summer. It can be somewhat sprawly and weedy.

Culture: Archangel does well in most soils under partial to full shade. If too leggy, it may be mowed at 15 to 20 cm (6 to 8 in.).

Use: It is best used as a ground cover, particularly under trees or on slopes where the vigorous underground stolons may be utilized to full advantage. Under border conditions it may become invasive.

Propagation: Lamiastrum is most easily propagated by division or terminal cuttings which root readily at the nodes.

Lamium maculatum 'Beacon Silver'

Gail Rankin

Lamium maculatum **'Beacon Silver'**
Spotted Deadnettle

Description: Although related to stinging nettles, the common name is derived from the fact that these plants have no such power, and because they lack the specialized hairs, are "dead". Similar to yellow archangel, spotted deadnettle is distinguished by its white, pink, or purple flowers. 'Beacon Silver' is characterized by silver leaves with green margins and pink hooded flowers on terminal stems in June or July. 'White Money' is similar but with white flowers.

Culture: They do best in evenly moist, well-drained soils in partial to full shade.

Use: They are particularly useful as a ground cover under shady conditions, even though they lack the trailing stems characteristic of *Lamiastrum*.

Propagation: Lamium is most easily propagated by division. As well, cuttings are readily rooted.

Lamium maculatum

Leontopodium alpinum
Alpine Edelweiss

Description: Native to the Swiss Alps , this is the plant popularized by the Broadway musical *The Sound of Music*. It has grey woolly leaves and grey-white, star-like flowers on 15 cm (6 in.) stems.

Under garden conditions it often appears drab. Various reasons have been set forth for its lack of appeal under cultivation. It is said to become whiter and brighter when associated with high-lime soils (which should not be a problem in most prairie regions). In Switzerland, they are reputed to grow under over-hanging cliffs; therefore planting in partial shade is recommended. Finally, there seems to be an enormous amount of variation in the plants themselves and sources of seed will differ.

Culture: Good drainage is essential! (Remember where they come from!) Plant in either full sun or partial shade.

Use: Edelweiss are useful in either the rock garden or the front of the border.

Propagation: Propagation is by seed or division.

Leontopodium alpinum

Leontopodium alpinum

Liatris

Liatris ligulistylis

Liatris
Gayfeather or Blazing Star

Description: Native to the great plains of North America, the gayfeathers produce spikes of purple to rose flowers in July. The tall gayfeather (*L. scariosa*) is 90 cm (3 ft.) while the spike gayfeather (*L. spicata*) is about 45 cm(18 in.). Both have attractive grass-like foliage. *Liatris ligulistylis* (meadow blazing star) is a fairly common native plant to moist places throughout the woodlands but is rare on the open prairie. One of the peculiarities of this plant that makes it different from most spikes is that it begins flowering from the top-most bud and moves downward.

Culture: Gayfeather grows best in ordinary, well-drained soils, in full sun. It may be chlorotic when grown in soils of high pH.

Use: Gayfeathers are a good addition to the border especially among pink or white flowers and are excellent in fresh and dried arrangements. An added bonus is that they attract butterflies.

Propagation: Propagation is through seed (chilled for several weeks) or division of the rhizomes in spring. It will sometimes self-seed but not to the point of invasiveness.

Ligularia vietchiana

Ligularia dentata (L. clivorum)
Ligularia or Elephant Ears

Description: The common name is an apt description of the huge rounded or kidney-shaped basal leaves. Tall [90 to 120 cm (3 to 4 ft.)] clusters or "flattened" spikes of yellow to orange flowers are produced in July and August. Two cultivars, 'Desdemona' and 'Othello' have orange flowers and leaves with purple undersides. Neither have been tested extensively in the prairie regions. Some very tall species [up to 3 m (6 to 7 ft.)] such as *L. vietchiana* can also be grown.

Culture: Ligularias do well under conditions of even moisture and will need a deep organic soil. Under hot prairie summers they will do better in full or partial shade. The leaves will show obvious wilting in hot sun. They are long-lived and non-invasive.

Use: They are excellent specimens for the shaded border or naturalized near a pond where moisture is plentiful.

Propagation: Propagation of named cultivars is by cutting or division in spring. Species plants may be produced from seed.

Ligularia dentata

Limonium spp.
Sea Lavender or Statice

Description: Two species of sea lavender do well in prairie gardens. Common or wide-leaf sea lavender (*Limonium latifolium*) has billowy sprays of tiny lavender blue flowers on 60 cm (2 ft.) stems in July and August. It is a long-lived perennial with dark green, leathery basal leaves and deep, penetrating roots. This is an excellent substitute for babysbreath. The cultivar 'Elegance' was rated hardy at Morden, Manitoba. German or tartarian statice, *Limonium tataricum* 'Angustifolium', (although sometimes listed as *Limonium dumosum*) blooms in July and August. Somewhat shorter, the flowers are similar but form flat-topped, triangular sprays which are silver-grey in color.

Culture: Both do well in a well-drained, sandy-loam soil in full sun with even moisture. Their common name, sea lavender, is derived from the fact that they are often used as sea-side plantings and are tolerant of saline soils and salty spray conditions. Clumps are best left undisturbed because of their deep tap roots.

Use: Both are excellent as border plants, fillers in cut flower arrangements, and are used extensively in dried arrangements as "everlastings."

Propagation: Propagation is by seed, root cuttings, or careful division. Seed germination is optimal under warm [21 to 24°C (70 to 75°F)], moist conditions.

Limonium latifolium

Limonium tataricum

Linum perenne

Linum perenne 'Alba'

Linum perenne

Linum spp.
Perennial Flax

Description: A native of Europe, flax was first grown as a fibre for use in linen and rope. Blue flax (*Linum perenne*) is 60 to 75 cm (24 to 30 in.) in height with narrow leaves and an airy appearance. Its small blue flowers [2.5 cm (1 in.) in diameter] bloom over a long period and combine well with other flowers. A white form (*Linum perenne* 'Alba') is also available. In shaded locations or on dull days the flowers will remain closed. Like daylilies, the individual flowers remain open for only one day, but are produced in such profusion that the plant is long blooming.

Linum flavum (golden flax) is only 30 to 38 cm (12 to 15 in.) high with blue green leaves. It is covered with bright yellow flowers in early summer.

Culture: Flax does well in most soils as long as drainage is adequate. It requires full sunlight.

Use: While the blue and white types are ideal for the mid-height range of the perennial border, the golden flax is best used at the front of the border or in the rock garden. Flax is also useful for naturalizing in drier or sandier locations. Because the flowers close when out of direct sunlight they are not suitable as cut flowers.

Propagation: Although relatively short-lived (three to four years) flax is easily grown from seed and will tend to self-sow in a non-mulched border where it may become weedy. Because of their woody crown, older plants do not transplant easily. They can also be propagated by cuttings taken in summer.

Lychnis chalcedonica
Maltese Cross

History: The species name is from Chalcedon, the ancient name of an area near Istanbul, Turkey, in which they are found. One legend says that these plants were brought back to Europe from Turkey by the Knights of Malta at the time of the Crusades.

Description: Maltese cross is an old fashioned garden perennial with bright green, opposite leaves and dense heads of scarlet flowers on 60 to 90 cm (2 to 3 ft.) stems in July. A white form is also available but is not as showy. Each floret composing the flower head resembles a cross.

Culture: It grows equally well in sun or partial shade in moist but well-drained soil.

Use: A good addition to the perennial border, it is also excellent as a cut flower.

Propagation: Maltese cross is easily propagated by seed or division. Do not cover the seeds as light is beneficial to their germination. Plants grown from seed will bloom their second year.

Lychnis haageana (Haages campion). Closely related to the Maltese cross, the Haages campion produces large orange-scarlet flowers on 30 cm (12 in.) stalks in July. Salmon and orange-red forms are also available. It requires even moisture.

Lychnis arkwrightii (the Arkwright campion). The Arkwright campion is a hybrid of *L. haageana* and *L. chalcedonica* with scarlet flowers the size of *L. haageana* and a height of 25 cm (10 in.). It blooms in July and is characterized by bronze-purple leaves. Unless given sheltered conditions it is not long-lived under prairie conditions.

Lychnis chalcedonica

Lychnis chalcedonica

Lychnis haageana

Lychnis coronaria

Lychnis coronaria

Lychnis coronaria
Rose Campion

Description: Often biennial in habit, the rose campion has light grey woolly leaves and sprays of contrasting bright carmine pink flowers. It is 60 to 90 cm (2 to 3 ft.) in height.

Culture: It does well in full sun with good drainage. Plants should be cut back after flowering.

Use: The carmine flowers go well with blues in the medium-height range of a border, and the grey foliage is a worthwhile addition to the border.

Propagation: It is best grown where it can self-sow and naturalize so that the bed as a whole can perpetuate itself.

Lychnis viscaria

Lychnis viscaria 'Splendens Flore-pleno'
Clammy Campion or Catchfly

Description: Closely resembling a carnation, the clammy campion has double, rose-magenta flowers and grassy foliage. It is 45 cm (18 in.) high and blooms in June or July.

The common name arises from the sticky stems. These plants were once hung from ceilings during an era which predated yellow fly paper – definitely an organic alternative!

Culture: It does well in full sun and well-drained soil.

Use: Catchfly is good in both the border and the rock garden.

Propagation: It is easily propagated by division.

Lychnis viscaria 'Splendens Flore-pleno'

Lysimachia nummularia
Moneywort or Creeping Jenny

Description: A prostrate or creeping plant, moneywort presents a picture of perpetual spring. It has small, rounded, opposite green leaves (said to resemble coins, hence the common name) and bright golden flowers in late spring. Roman farmers were said to have placed the flowers under the yokes of their oxen as an insect repellent. Only 5 cm (2 in.) high, the stems root at the nodes as they grow. It may become invasive.

Culture: Moneywort does well in sun or shade but prefers even moisture. The golden leaf cultivar (*Lysimachia nummularia* 'Aurea') is less vigorous and does better in partial shade.

Use: It is excellent as a groundcover, for edging, or naturalized in a moist setting.

Propagation: Propagation is by division or cuttings.

Lysimachia nummularia

Lysimachia nummularia

Lythrum sp.

Lythrum 'Morden Pink'

Lythrum sp.

Lythrum spp.
Lythrum or Loosestrife

Note: Purple lythrum (*Lythrum salicaria*), a native of Europe introduced in the 1800s, became a naturalized weed in wetland areas of the eastern United States and Canada, choking out much of the native wetland vegetation. In recent years, however, it has spread across the entire continent. Since this book was first published, it has become apparent that the less aggressive species and even the horticultural cultivars that are unable to produce viable seed can cross-pollinate with their wild loosestrife cousins and produce viable seed. Therefore Loosestrife is no longer recommended as a garden perennial and is in fact declared a noxious weed in many parts of the continent.

Description: The following cultivars are the safest to grow in areas of the continent where this plant has not been outlawed. All are hardy and bloom from July to September.

'Morden Pink' was first introduced in 1937. A bud sport of *L. virgatum*, it is 120 cm (4 ft.) in height and pure pink.

Both 'Morden Gleam' and 'Morden Rose' are the result of crosses between 'Morden Pink' and *L. alatum*.' Morden Gleam' is a vigorous plant of 120 cm (4 ft.) with rosy pink flowers. It is characterized by many side branches which tend to prolong its blooming period. 'Morden Rose' is a compact plant of 90 cm (3 ft.) with dark foliage and rosy red flowers. It is more tolerant of hot, dry weather.

'Dropmore Purple' is 90 cm (3 ft.) in height with deep purple flowers. It is a hybrid of *L. salicaria* and *L. virgatum* developed by the late Dr. F. Skinner of Dropmore, Manitoba.

'Mr. Robert' is a compact plant of only 60 to 90 cm (2 to 3 ft.) with bright pink flowers.

Culture: Lythrums do better under conditions of even moisture, although some cultivars are tolerant of drier conditions once they are established. They do well in ordinary garden loam enriched with peat moss in full sun or partial shade. They are best planted in the spring with the dormant buds or "eyes" 5 cm (2 in.) below the soil surface. Pinching the stems in spring will produce bushier plants.

Use: Lythrum make excellent border plants, do well when naturalized in wet areas or around ponds, and are excellent as short-term cut flowers.

Propagation: Cuttings should be taken from the base of the plants when 8 to 10 cm (3 to 4 in.) high. Place them in moist vermiculite or perlite in indirect light until rooted, usually about three weeks. The roots are woody and difficult to divide.

Malva moschata
Musk Mallow

Description: Mallow is a somewhat sprawling plant of 90 to 120 cm (3 to 4 ft.) with rosy-pink flowers on terminal and side spikes similar to those of hollyhock. It blooms in mid-summer. It tends to be short-lived but reseeds.

Culture: Mallows require full sun and good drainage.

Use: They are a useful plant toward the back of a larger border or for hiding unsightly objects.

Propagation: Propagation is by seed (which may be sown directly where the plants are to be grown) or by division.

Malva moschata

Matteuccia struthiopteris pensylvanica
Ostrich Fern

Description: One of the largest ferns found in North America, ostrich ferns form graceful clumps of fronds (finely divided leaves) 90 to 120 cm (3 to 4 ft.) in height. They have no flowers. Fertile fronds (leaves containing spores) will occasionally arise from the center of the clump. These tend to be shorter, more erect, darker in color and less attractive than the "normal" sterile fronds. A specialized means of reproduction, they do the plant neither harm nor good and can be removed if considered undesirable.

Culture: Ostrich ferns do well under conditions of shade, even moisture, an organic soil, and shelter from the wind.

Use: Ferns are ideal for the shade garden, the north side of the building (as long as the soil is moist and it is a sheltered position), or naturalized where shade and moisture are plentiful.

Propagation: Propagation is by division or by spores. Under favorable conditions the roots may be long and somewhat invasive.

Matteuccia struthiopteris pensylvanica

Mertensia paniculata

Mertensia paniculata

Mertensia virginica
Virginia Bluebells

Description: Virginia bluebells are one of the loveliest of the early spring-flowering perennials. Sixty cm (2 ft.) in height, they produce nodding clusters of bells which are reddish-purple when in bud, but change to gentian blue as the flowers open. The foliage dies to the ground by midsummer. In shaded areas of the perennial border they should be planted adjacent to later-flowering spreading plants such as the cranesbill geraniums.

A similar species, native to much of northern North America, is tall lungwort, *Mertensia paniculata*.

Culture: They prefer a rich, moist, organic soil and partial or full shade.

Use: Virginia bluebells are excellent for naturalizing or for the wild garden.

Propagation: Propagation is by division once they become dormant or by seed which should be sown immediately after collection.

Monarda spp.
Bee Balm, Bergamot, Oswego Tea

History: John Bartram, the plant explorer who first introduced *Monarda* to Europe, found them at Oswego, an outpost on Lake Ontario, where it was used for tea - hence the common name: Oswego Tea.

Description: A member of the mint family, *Monarda* produces round thistle-like heads of mauve, red, or white flowers on stems of 60 to 90 cm (2 to 3 ft.). The leaves are aromatic. 'Minnedosa' is a white form native to the Canadian prairies. 'Neepawa', 'Souris', and 'Wawanesa' have pink to purple flowers and have emerged from the Canadian prairie breeding programs. 'Marshall's Delight' is a more recent introduction with resistance to powdery mildew. It is 65 cm (25 in.) in height with pink flowers and light green leaves.

Monarda fistulosa

They bloom in July. In some parts of the prairie region the hybrids are considered only marginally hardy if planted in other than a sheltered location. If they survive more than three years, they may become invasive.

Culture: Because of their susceptibility to powdery mildew, bee balms need well-drained soil, full sun, and good air circulation. Avoid wetting the foliage when watering. After flowering, remove the spent blooms for a neater appearance. New basal leaves should soon form.

Use: Bee balm makes a good border plant, attracts both bees and hummingbirds, and is also useful as a cut flower. It will naturalize in a wild garden.

Propagation: Propagation of the hybrids is by spring division.

Monarda

Myosotis sylvatica
Forget-Me-Not

Description: A true biennial, the forget-me-not produces only foliage during its first season of growth, and flowers, sets seed, and dies during its second year. But because they flower continually during their second year (in much the same way as annuals), seed set early in the season will germinate during the same season, and thus the planting as a whole will continue to perpetuate itself, although each individual plant will only survive two years.

The flowers are light blue with a yellow eye and are held above graceful mounds of foliage 30 to 38 cm (12 to 15 in.) in height. They bloom most profusely during May and June and then sporadically the remainder of the summer. Improved cultivars such as 'Victoria Blue' or 'Blue Ball' are available.

Myosostis alpestris (alpine forget-me-not) is a true perennial but rarely is seen in gardens. It is only 15 cm (6 in.) in height and native to the Arctic.

Myosotis sylvatica

Myosotis alpestris

Culture: Forget-me-nots do well in full or partial shade in ordinary soil with even moisture.

Use: They are excellent for naturalizing under open trees or woodlands where moisture is adequate. They are charming along with white anemones *(Anemone sylvestris)* under plum or apple trees.

Propagation: Propagation is by seed.

Nepeta mussinii

Nepeta

Nepeta x *ucranica* 'Dropmore'
Catmint

History: 'Dropmore' catmint, developed by the late Dr. Frank Skinner, of Manitoba, Canada, is a hybrid of *N. mussinii* and *N. ucranica* and was first listed in Skinner's catalogue in 1932.

Description: It is a compact plant of 30 to 38 cm (12 to 15 in.) with attractive, scalloped gray-green leaves and light purple flowers from May to September . Unlike most members of the mint family, it is not invasive. The foliage contains oils which are attractive to cats, hence the common name. (If you dislike cats, it is an excellent gift for a neighbor!)

Culture: They grow well in full sun or partial shade in well-drained soil and are tolerant of neglect.

Use: Catmint is useful in the border, the herb garden, and as a cut flower.

Propagation: Propagation is by division or cuttings.

Oenothera missouriensis
Ozark Sundrop or Missouri Evening Primrose

Description: The Missouri evening primrose produces pale yellow, tissue paper-like flowers from July onward. The decorative winged seed pods are useful in dried arrangements. The stems are 45 cm (18 in.) high and somewhat floppy or trailing.

Culture: They prefer full sun and ordinary, well-drained soil. They tend to be drought tolerant once established.

Use: The Missouri evening primrose is best naturalized as part of a wild prairie garden.

Propagation: They are easily grown from seed and tend to self-seed.

Oenothera missouriensis

Oenothera missouriensis

Opuntia polyacantha
Prickly Pear Cactus

Description: A native to the prairies, the prickly pear cactus is about 12 cm (5 in.) in height and produces waxy, lemon yellow flowers in mid-summer. As the name implies, it is both pear-shaped and prickly! The fruit is an edible berry.

Culture: It will flourish on a dry hillside on sandy soil in full sun. Under normal garden conditions it will soon rot.

Opuntia polyacantha

Opuntia polyacantha

Use: This is an ideal candidate for the hotter, drier areas of a rock garden but only if the location is inaccessible to pets and small children!

Propagation: Propagate with care! They may be increased by seed or simply by rooting the fleshy segments in moist sand.

Brian Porter

Paeonia sp.

Ed Toop

Paeonia sp.

W E Smith

Paeonia spp.
Peony

Description: Peonies are among the showiest and most long-lived of all perennials. Many still flourish in prairie homesteads which have long been abandoned. They are available in single through anemone to double flowered types and range in height from 45 to 90 cm (18 in. to 3 ft.). Colors range from white to pink to red and include a creamy yellow fading to white. Hundreds of cultivars are available. Among those recommended are 'Karl Rosenfeld', 'Felix Crousse', 'Red Charm' (double, red); 'Sarah Bernhardt' and 'Monsieur Jules Elie' (double, pink); 'Festiva Maxima' (fragrant, double, white); 'Laura Dessert' (fragrant, anemone, pale yellow); 'Peter Barr' (red, single); and the fern leaf peony (*P. tenuifolia*). The latter has extremely fine-cut leaves and blooms very early and is available in both single and double-flowered forms in pink or red. Tree peonies (*P. suffruticosa*) are not reliably hardy in the prairie region.

Note: the foliage of the fern leaf peonies yellows and dies back in midsummer.

Culture: Peonies do best in full sun with good drainage. Once established, they are remarkably drought tolerant. Many of the older, double-flowered varieties will require support when in bloom due to the weight of the flowers and the relative weakness of the stems. Wire hoops are available for this purpose commercially or can be made at home.

They are best planted and divided in the fall. Each fleshy root division should contain three to five pink buds or "eyes". Dig the holes deep enough so that the roots will not be crowded. Thoroughly incorporate peat moss into the existing soil. Do not add fertilizer or manure to the planting hole. Set the roots so that the buds will be covered with no more than 5 cm (2 in.) of soil. Deeper planting delays bloom while shallower planting makes the buds more vulnerable to winter damage. Firm the soil and water well.

Peonies are sometimes affected by a fungal disease called botrytis or "peony blight" which causes the buds to turn brown or black. The base of the stems becomes black or grey. Diseased plants should be drenched with a systemic fungicide according to label directions. The foliage of diseased plants should be cut and removed in the fall to prevent spores from overwintering.

Note: contrary to garden folklore the presence of ants on the plant is neither harmful to the peony nor necessary to its well-being. The ants are simply after the proverbial "free lunch" (attracted to the exuded sugars on the flower buds).

Use: They are excellent border plants, used either singly or massed, useful as hedges, and are invaluable as cut flowers.

Propagation: Propagation is most commonly achieved through division but they may also be raised from seed which should be sown as soon as it is ripe. Either way may take four or more years for plants to produce blooms characteristic of the variety.

Paeonia tenuifolia 'Lacinata'

Paeonia sp.

Papaver nudicaule
Iceland Poppy

Description: The Iceland poppy is a dainty plant with long slender stems [30 to 38 cm (12 to 15 in.)] bearing flowers in shades of orange, yellow, white, cream, and salmon pink. Their texture is like tissue paper. Unlike the Oriental poppies, they produce bloom over almost the entire summer. However, they are shorter lived and tend to behave more like a biennial. Because they readily self-seed, the planting as a whole remains permanent as long as it is not mulched.

Culture: Like other poppies, Iceland poppies prefer full sun and well-drained soil and are drought resistant.

Papaver nudicaule

Papaver nudicaule

Use: Because of their long blooming period Iceland poppies are excellent when massed in the perennial border or rock garden. They may also be used as cut flowers.

Propagation: Although they are easily grown from seed, they are somewhat difficult to transplant due to their tap root. They are best seeded in individual biodegradable peat pots or sown directly where they are to be grown.

Papaver orientale 'Pink Lassie'

Gail Rankin

Papaver orientale

Sara Williams

Papaver orientale
Oriental Poppy

History: The word "poppy" is from the Anglo-Saxon word "popig" which means sleep. Certain species were used to make a drink which induced sleepiness. "Pap" means "milky juice".

Description: Oriental poppies are available in white, pink, salmon, orange, and red, in both single and double forms, with flowers ranging from 10 to 15 cm (4 to 6 in.) in diameter. They bloom in June. The plants are usually about 60 cm (2 ft.) high. The leaves are large, hairy and divided, and the sap is milky.

Culture: Poppies need a well drained soil in full sun. Protection from the wind as well as digging in organic matter is beneficial. When planting, set the roots straight down. Mulch for the first winter, but take care not to cover the rosette of new leaves with the mulch.

Oriental poppies should be divided and transplanted in August after they have flowered and when the foliage has dried up but prior to the production of a new rosette of leaves. This needs to be done only once every five years.

Use: Although they make a dramatic impact in the perennial border when in bloom, after flowering the foliage becomes shabby as the flower stems and lower leaves die. For this reason they are best planted behind later flowering plants such as perennial asters, chrysanthemums, babysbreath or some of the cranesbill geraniums. Planting poppies in diagonal "drifts" or singly will further help to disguise the dying foliage.

Poppies make excellent cut flowers and will last longer if cut early in the morning just as the buds are about to open. The seed pod is both decorative and useful as a "stamp" in craft work if first applied to an ordinary colored stamp ink pad.

Propagation: Poppies may be propagated by seed or root cuttings. The seed is extremely fine. Prior to sowing it should be placed in a freezer for 48 hours to break dormancy. It should be sowed thinly and barely pressed into the soil. Although it is recommended that the seeds be germinated in complete darkness, some growers have not found this necessary. Poppy seedlings will usually need several transplantings before they can be moved outdoors.

Poppies may also be grown from 5 cm (2 in.) portions of root, about pencil thickness or slightly thicker. These should be taken in August before new growth starts. Set them horizontally about 8 cm (3 in.) deep in a cold frame. They should send up shoots the same fall or the following spring.

Small plants often develop around the edge of an old plant after flowering and these can be transplanted as new healthy plants.

Papaver orientale

Penstemon spp.
Beard Tongue

Description: Why the name beard tongue? Of the five stamens contained in the flower, one is sterile and often bearded, hence the common name.

Native to much of North America, including the prairie regions, some of the *Penstemon* species as well as the hybrid cultivars have proved hardy under prairie conditions. The two-lipped tubular flowers are produced in terminal racemes in mid-summer in shades of white, pink, blue, and purple. Most are 30 to 90 cm (1 to 3 ft.) in height. Among those recommended are the smooth beard tongue (*P. glaber*), the shell leaf penstemon (*P. grandiflorus*) and the torrey penstemon (*P. barbatus torreyi*). 'Prairie Dawn' and 'Prairie Dusk' are hybrids introduced from Nebraska.

Culture: All *Penstemons* thrive in full sun in well-drained soil.

Penstemon procerus

Hugh Knowles

Penstemon sp.

Use: The taller beard tongues are attractive in the perennial border while the dwarf cultivars fit in well in the rock garden. They are also useful for naturalizing in a prairie garden and as cut flowers.

Propagation: They are propagated by seed, cuttings, and spring division.

Phalaris arundinacea var. *picta*

Phalaris arundinacea **var.** *picta*
Ribbon Grass

Description: Ribbon grass is usually 60 to 120 cm (2 to 4 ft.) high with striped white and green leaves 15 to 30 cm (6 to 12 in.) long and 2 cm (0.75 in.) wide. The flowers are insignificant.

Note: Hardy brome grasses which are somewhat similar include a selection of *Bromus inermis* called 'Gay Bouquet' which has pink and green variegations and 'Skinner's Golden' which has yellow variegations.

Culture: It does well in well drained soil in full sun but will tolerate poorer, drier soils and partial shade.

Use: It is useful as a ground cover in full sun or an understory in partial shade. It is too aggressive for the border unless contained in a sunken pot.

Propagation: Propagation is by division.

Phalaris arundinacea var. *picta*

Phlox spp.
Dwarf Phloxes

Description: This group of low, mat-forming, early spring blooming phloxes is made up of several species and hybrids. *Phlox borealis* (Arctic phlox) , native to Alaska, has evergreen leaves and bright pink flowers. *Phlox hoodii* (Hood's phlox) is a mainly white species, only 2.5 cm (1 in.) high, native to the prairie grasslands of much of North America. *Phlox subulata* (moss phlox) produces white, pink, lavender blue, or rosy red flowers. Its foliage takes on a bronzy green appearance toward autumn and is somewhat prickly. Its cultivars include 'Atropurpurea' (purple), 'Rosea' (rose), 'G F Wilson' (mauve), 'Fairy' (compact pale mauve) and 'Temiscaming' (rosy red). The blue and white types, including 'Emerald Cushion Blue' seem less adapted to unsheltered prairie conditions.

Culture: Dwarf phlox do well in full sun and well drained soil. Unlike the taller phlox, the dwarf phlox will tolerate poor soil and some drought. Because the bright green foliage is evergreen, if snow cover is inadequate, or if it is planted in a windy, exposed area, some browning and dieback may occur. Conversely, they have been reported to suffer from snow mould under heavy snow cover in some areas. Because new growth may emerge from foliage that appears "dead," it is advisable not to prune off the "dead" material until early June. Shearing after flowering promotes a more compact plant.

Use: These plants are excellent for edging or used among low, evergreen shrubs. They are ideal for the rock garden or as a ground cover.

Propagation: Propagation is by division and cuttings.

Phlox subulata

Phlox subulata

Phlox subulata 'Emerald Cushion Blue'

Three cultivars of *Phlox paniculata*
'Widar', 'Antonin Mercier', 'Aida'

Ed Toop

Saskatchewan Department of Agriculture & Food

Phlox carolina 'White Pyramid'

Phlox carolina (P. suffruticosa)
Carolina Phlox

Description: Several cultivars of the Carolina phlox have proven hardy in the prairie region. Most flower in July and August. Both 'Ada Blackjack' and 'Moose Jaw' are 75 cm (30 in.) in height with rose pink flowers usually in July. 'White Pyramid' is 90 cm (3 ft.) in height with white flowers in July. The plants remain compact and nonaggressive. The summer perennial phlox (*P. paniculata*) has tested only medium hardy at trials in central Canada.

There appears to be confusion in the trade between the two species. *Phlox paniculata* is found in the wild from New York to Georgia and Arkansas whereas *Phlox carolina* is native from Ohio to Florida. Some of the cultivars given above may be listed as cultivars of *P. paniculata* in some catalogues.

Culture: Phlox does best in full sun in an organic, loamy soil which is well drained but evenly moist.

Use: These are excellent plants for the perennial border and for cutting.

Propagation: Propagation is by division or by root cuttings.

Physalis alkekengi

Physalis alkekengi (P. franchetii)
Chinese Lantern

Description: A member of the potato family, Chinese lanterns are grown for their bright, papery, pumpkin-orange seed pods which are said to resemble lanterns. The small white flowers are insignificant and usually hidden by the leaves. The plants themselves are 60 cm (2 ft.) high and spread by underground stolons which can be somewhat invasive.

Culture: They do well in sun or shade in ordinary soil with even moisture (especially as the lanterns are developing).

Use: The seed pods, produced in September, are widely used for dried arrangements. Because Chinese lanterns lack ornamental value through much of the growing season, they are usually relegated to the reserve border.

Propagation: They may be grown from seed but are most easily propagated by division. Seed should be chilled for a few months in the refrigerator prior to sowing.

Physostegia virginiana
Obedient Plant, Lion's Heart or False Dragonhead

Physostegia virginiana

Description: The obedient plant produces dense spikes of pink tubular flowers resembling snapdragons on 60 cm (2 ft.) stems in late summer. A white form is also available, but may not be as hardy as the pink. The common name refers to the fact that the individual flowers which form the spike are on hinged stalks which can be angled for specific flower arrangements and will remain in the position in which they are placed. A variegated foliage form also exists.

Culture: They do well in sun or partial shade in most soils.

Use: Obedient plants are valued both in the border and in arrangements. As cut flowers, they are fairly long lasting. In the border they bloom over a long period when many other perennials are not in flower. They can be invasive (disobedient plant?) and should not be allowed to over-run other less vigorous perennials. They may be naturalized in moist locations.

Propagation: Propagation is by division and seed.

Physostegia virginiana 'Morden Beauty'

Platycodon grandiflorum

Platycodon grandiflorum

Platycodon grandiflorum
Balloonflower

Description: A relative of the bellflowers, the balloonflower is a long-lived, tidy perennial which blooms in July and August. The common name is derived from the fact that, prior to opening, the flower bud swells up, resembling a balloon. Once open, they are broadly bell-shaped. The blue flowers are produced on 60 cm (2 ft.) stems. A white form, 'Album', and a pink form, 'Roseum', are also available and are reliably hardy. The pink flowered types prefer partial shade.

Culture: Balloonflowers should be planted in full sun or partial shade in a well-drained, sandy loam soil. Because the stems emerge from the soil later than most perennials it is advisable to label them so as not to inadvertently hoe them off. Plants take as long as three years to reach an acceptable size.

Use: Balloonflowers make attractive border plants, blooming over a long period. They are also long-lasting as cut flowers.

Propagation: They are easily grown from seed or careful spring division of the fleshy root. When planting or dividing, set the crowns about 2.5 cm (1 in.) below soil level. Outer divisions of the original crown are more likely to be successfully transplanted.

Polemonium caeruleum

Polemonium caeruleum
Jacob's Ladder

Description: Cultivated since Roman times, Jacob's ladder has attractive pinnate leaves and panicles of open, bell-like, blue flowers with orange stamens on 60 cm (2 ft.) stems in June and July. The individual leaflets which make up the compound leaf are supposed to resemble the ladder on which angels ascended in Jacob's dream in the Old Testament.

The skunk leaf polemonium (*P. pulcherrimum*) is similar but shorter. Creeping polemonium (*P. reptans*) is 30 cm (12 in.) in height with blue flowers. Both have proved hardy in trials at Morden, Manitoba, in Canada.

Culture: They grow best in moist soil and partial shade.

Use: An excellent plant for the front of the border, it can also be naturalized in a shady woodland garden.

Propagation: Jacob's ladder is easily propagated by seed, division, or cuttings taken in mid-summer.

Polemonium caeruleum

Polygonatum multiflorum
Eurasian Solomon's Seal

Description: Solomon's seal is 75 cm (30 in.) in height with tall, arching stems bearing nodding white bells edged in green. It flowers in June. Blue-black berries follow. The common name refers to the cross-section of the root which is said to resemble King Solomon's seal, a six-pointed star. *Polygonatum odoratum*, the fragrant solomon's seal, has proven hardy in central Canada.

Note: this plant is different from the native plants, false solomon's seal (*Smilacina stellata*), which has flowers borne in loose terminal spikes, and wild lily-of-the-valley or two-leaved solomon's seal (*Maianthemum canadense*) which has denser more upright flower spikes and only two leaves.

Culture: They do well in moist, shady areas in soil enriched with organic matter.

Use: Solomon's seal is excellent in a shade garden, naturalized in a wild garden, and as a cut flower. The foliage alone makes it a worthwhile plant.

Propagation: Propagation is by spring division or seed. Seed should be chilled for 6 to 8 weeks prior to sowing.

Polygonatum multiflorum

Polygonatum multiflorum

Polygonum

Polygonum

Polygonum bistorta
Knotweed or Fleeceflower

Description: Not a common plant, knotweed has proven hardy enough to be grown successfully in prairie gardens. Spikes of light pink flowers on 60 cm (2 ft.) stems are produced in early spring. They resemble a bottle brush or short poker. The plants form clumps with large, dark green leaves with a distinctive white midrib.

Culture: They thrive in full sun or partial shade as long as the soil is evenly moist.

Use: Knotweed is an excellent candidate for pond or waterside plantings and will also do well in shade gardens as long as moisture is plentiful. The flowers are long-lasting when cut.

Propagation: Propagation is by seed or spring division.

Potentilla spp.
Cinquefoil

Description: Members of the rose family, potentillas, both herbaceous and woody forms, are distinguished by their five-petaled, buttercup-like flowers and strawberry-like leaves. The flowers are usually yellow, cream, white, or orange-red, with a strong flush of bloom in June with sporadic flowering the remainder of the summer. The plants range in height from a few centimetres up to 60 cm (2 ft.) .

Although the herbaceous potentillas have not been tested extensively in different prairie locations, many have survived successfully in the prairie environment. There is some confusion in nomenclature.

Potentilla alpestre (orangespot cinquefoil) has been available for decades from Skinners Nursery in Dropmore, Manitoba,

Potentilla alpestre

Canada. It is 30 to 35 cm (12 to 15 in.) high with orange-yellow flowers in June and July and ruggedly hardy.

Potentilla anserina (silverweed) is only 15 cm (6 in.) high and forms a thick, spreading ground cover with yellow flowers in May and June. A yellow flowered type with pompom-like flowers forms an even thicker mat.

Potentilla grandiflora is 38 cm (15 in.) high with bright yellow flowers in July on more upright plants.

Potentilla recta (sulfur cinquefoil) is 75 cm (2.5 ft.) high with pale yellow flowers from June to August. It is rated as marginally hardy but considered a useful border plant.

Potentilla atrosanguinea (Himalayan cinquefoil) is 45 cm (18 in.) high with a mound-like form, silky, grey leaves and bright red flowers. Although rated as "tender" at trials in central Canada, it has been grown successfully in the region if sheltered conditions are provided.

Potentilla tridentata (three-toothed cinquefoil) is 5 to 30 cm (2 to 12 in.) in height with dark, evergreen, lustrous leaves and white flowers. It is excellent as a ground cover in difficult areas.

Potentilla glandulosa is 45 to 60 cm (1.5 to 2 ft.) in height with flowers from pale yellow to creamy white.

Culture: Cinquefoils do well in full sun in well-drained soils. Most are drought tolerant.

Use: They are ideal subjects for the rock garden or as ground covers in hot dry areas which cannot be watered.

Propagation: Propagation is by seed or division.

Potentilla 'Goldrush'

Potentilla anserina

Primula auricula

Primula auricula

Primula cortusoides

Gail Rankin (vertical, right of first image)

Alberta Horticultural Association (vertical, right of second image)

Brian Porter (vertical, right of third image)

Primula spp.
Primrose

Description: Primroses are among the earliest spring-blooming perennials. Of low stature, they are available in a wide range of color and form.

The auricula or dusty miller primrose (*P. auricula*), the cortusa primrose (*P. cortusoides*), and *Primula* 'Assiniboine' have all proved reliably hardy throughout the Canadian prairies. The drumstick primrose (*P. denticulata*) and the siebold primrose (*P. sieboldii*) will survive under more sheltered conditions with adequate snow cover.

Primula 'Assiniboine'. This is a very hardy hybrid of *P. pallasi* x *P. officinale* which was introduced by the late Dr. Frank Skinner of Dropmore, Manitoba, Canada, in 1965. It is still available from Skinner's Nursery. Extremely rugged, 'Assiniboine' grows in the open garden or in partial shade. It has peach-colored petals and a yellow eye, is about 30 cm (12 in.) high and blooms in May.

Primula auricula (dusty miller primrose). Native to the Alps of Europe, and reliably hardy, the auricula or dusty miller primrose has mealy green leaves from which the common name dusty miller is derived. It is said to resemble flour sprinkled on the apron of a miller. The flowers have yellow "eyes" with either yellow, red, lavender, purple, or red petals. They are 30 to 38 cm (12 to 15 in.) high and bloom in May. Auriculas have proven reliably hardy for decades in prairie gardens with no extra protection. They are more tolerant of partially sunny conditions than most primroses and are easily propagated by seed or crown division. They do not tend to self-seed.

Primula cortusoides (cortusa primrose). The hardy cortusa primrose has a basal rosette of light green "wrinkled" leaves with attractive pink flowers held above the foliage on 30 cm (12 in.) stems. It blooms in May and again in September. Large clumps may be carefully divided by gently teasing apart, but this is seldom necessary as the cortusa primrose self-seeds or "naturalizes" very easily, given moist shady conditions. It is one of the primroses least tolerant of hot dry conditions and will soon wilt if placed in direct sunlight. A native of Siberia, it, too, is considered reliably hardy.

Primula denticulata (drumstick or Himalayan primrose). Hardy in some areas of prairie Canada, the drumstick primrose is nevertheless classified as marginally hardy. For this reason, it is best planted in a sheltered location in which it will be assured maximum snow cover. Further hardiness testing is needed. The individual flowers are 1.3 cm (0.5 in.) in diameter and form rounded flower heads (which are said to resemble "drumsticks") in lilac, violet, or white, on 25 cm (10 in.) stalks. The white flowered form is supposed to breed true from seed. The drumstick primrose is native to the Himalayas.

Primula sieboldii (siebold primrose). A native of Japan, the siebold primrose has been successfully grown in some areas of the prairies. Only 23 cm (9 in.) high, the flowers are available in white, rose, or purple, and are about 4 cm (1.5 in.) in diameter. Like other primroses, it demands even moisture. This particular one is recommended for pond-side gardens and will withstand more sun than others. Further hardiness testing is needed.

Primula x *polyanthus* (polyanthus primrose). A large group of hybrids resulting from intercrosses of *P. veris*, *P. elatoir*, and *P. vulgaris*, the polyanthus primroses are of variable hardiness. They might survive in a more sheltered location with dependable snow cover. Further hardiness testing is needed.

Culture: Primroses do well in shady locations with even moisture. Adding peat moss to the soil is recommended to increase the soils' water-holding capacity.

Use: They are ideal used *en masse* in a shady border, near a pond or water garden or naturalized in a moist, shady location.

Propagation: Primroses are easily grown from seed which should be sown as soon as it ripens. Some seed will require a cold treatment before germination occurs. Others will readily "naturalize" through self-seeding. Most are easily divided.

Primula sp.

Primula sp.

Primula sp.

Pulmonaria officinalis

Olds College Collection

Pulmonaria saccharata

Olds College Collection

Pulmonaria spp.
Lungwort

History: The common name is derived from the fact that these plants were once thought to cure lung problems. In the 1400s it was believed that a plant's physical appearance suggested its medicinal use. Thus, the spotted leaves were compared to diseased lungs.

Description: Several species of lungwort have proven hardy at trials in central Canada. All are about 30 cm (12 in.) in height and produce clusters of nodding, bell-like flowers in June. They are long lived and non-invasive.

Pulmonaria angustifolia (cowslip lungwort) has blue flowers and dark green leaves. The common lungwort (*P. officinalis*) is larger with violet buds opening to blue and leaves blotched with white. It is the most easily naturalized of the three species described here. Bethlehem sage (*P. saccharata*) has violet flowers and more heavily spotted silver leaves which are pointed at both ends. It appears to be less hardy than the other two species and will do better in a sheltered location.

Culture: All lungworts prefer an evenly moist, organic soil in full or partial shade.

Use: Use as specimen plants, massed in shady, moist areas, or in the shade garden. The foliage alone is attractive.

Propagation: Lungworts are propagated by seed, division after flowering, or root cuttings.

Ranunculus acris

Gail Rankin

Ranunculus acris 'Flore Pleno'
Tall Buttercup or Yellow Bachelor's Button

Description: Sixty centimetres (2 ft.) in height, the tall buttercup has small, double, yellow flowers (resembling buttons) from late June to October. The leaves are deeply lobed.

Culture: They do well in sun or partial shade in ordinary soil, but will perform better with even moisture.

Use: The tall buttercup is useful for the mid-range of the border or naturalizing.

Propagation: Propagation is by seed or division.

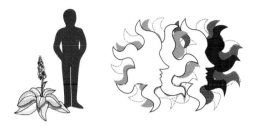

Ranunculus acris

Olds College Collection

Rheum palmatum
Ornamental Rhubarb

Description: Resembling its edible cousin, but on a much larger scale, the ornamental rhubarb produces red or creamy flowers on stalks up to 2 m (6 ft.) in height in mid-summer. The dark green leaves are deeply lobed and form large basal clumps.

Culture: It does well in ordinary soil in full sun or partial shade.

Use: This plant embodies the true meaning of a "bold accent plant" and is useful in a large perennial border or as a waterside planting. In a smaller garden it will be totally out of scale.

Propagation: Propagation is by division.

Rheum palmatum

University of Alberta Plant Science Collection

Rheum palmatum

Saskatchewan Department of Agriculture & Food

Rudbeckia laciniata
Coneflower or Goldenglow

Rudbeckia 'Gloriosa Daisy'

Sara Williams

Description: The most reliable of the coneflowers is goldenglow which reaches a height of 150 cm (5 ft.) and has large, yellow, double flowers in August and September. It usually does not require staking.

Culture: It does well in evenly moist soil and full sun.

Use: Goldenglow is useful toward the back of a large border or for hiding unsightly objects. It also makes a long-lasting cut flower.

Propagation: It is easily propagated by division in early spring.

Note: another well-known coneflower, the gloriosa daisy (*R. hirta*), will usually bloom the first year from seed but will seldom over-winter. It should be treated as an annual.

Rudbeckia

Olds College Collection

Salvia **spp.**
Meadow Sage

Salvia pratensis

Description: Of the sages tested in Canada, only the *Salvia pratensis* (meadow sage) has proven reliably hardy. Growers in some parts of the prairie region have reported it to be less reliable. It has large, dark green leaves and blue or white tubular flowers produced in whorls on 60 to 90 cm (2 to 3 ft.) stems in June. Like other members of the mint family, the stems are square and the leaves are opposite. It is somewhat biennial in habit so seedlings should be saved.

Salvia x *suberba* (violet sage) is a hybrid which is hardy, drought resistant, long-blooming and beautiful – altogether, a first-rate plant. It is 60 to 90 cm (2 to 3 ft.) in height, has grey-green, aromatic foliage and dense flower heads. Cultivars include 'Blue Queen', 'Pink Queen' and 'May Night'.

Culture: Salvias grow best in full sun, in soil which has been enriched with organic material, and is evenly moist but well drained.

Use: They are well suited to the sunny perennial border, especially when massed. They are also useful as both fresh cut flowers and for dried arrangements.

Propagation: Salvia is easily propagated from seed and will self-seed under favorable conditions. It can also be grown from division in early spring or by terminal cuttings. Division can be difficult because of the woody nature of the root stock.

Sanguinaria canadensis
Bloodroot

Description: Bloodroot is a native of eastern North America bearing pure white flowers on 15 cm (6 in.) stems in May. The kidney-shaped leaves are very attractive, scalloped and bluish-green. A double-flowered form is also available.

Both the common and generic names are derived from the fact that sap from the root is blood red and was once used as a dye and as body paint.

Culture: It does best in shaded, evenly moist soil to which a generous amount of organic matter has been added.

Use: It is an excellent plant for a shade garden or a woodland setting.

Propagation: Propagation is by division after flowering or seed. Given favorable conditions it will self-sow.

Ed Topp

Sanguinaria canadensis

Olds College Collection

Sanguinaria canadensis

Saponaria ocymoides

University of Alberta Plant Science Collection

Saponaria ocymoides

Olds College Collection

Saponaria ocymoides
Rock Soapwort

Description: The rock soapwort is about 15 cm (6 in.) high and produces star-shaped, pink flowers on trailing stems in June. The name "soapwort" comes from the fact that the leaves and roots of some species lather and have been used as a soap substitute.

Note: *Saponaria officinalis* is also hardy but is too weedy to be recommended for a perennial border.

Culture: They do well in well-drained soil in full sun. Shearing after flowering will help maintain a more compact form.

Use: Rock soapwort is an excellent plant for the rockery.

Propagation: Propagation is by division in spring, cuttings taken in late summer, or seed (which should be chilled for 4 to 6 weeks prior to sowing).

Gail Rankin

Saxifraga x *walpole*

Saxifraga spp.
Saxifrage

Description: The genus name, *Saxifraga*, means "breaker of rocks" and refers to the ability of the seed to germinate in rock crevices, giving the illusion that this humble plant was responsible for the crack.

The saxifrage form a large group of plants known for their attractive foliage; neat, tuft-like form; and dainty flowers. There is some confusion over the names of these plants and many are poorly labeled when sold. Few have been extensively tested for hardiness. In spite of these problems, they are worthy of trial and many should prove hardy. *Saxifraga paniculata* (*S. aizoon*) has neat mounds of bright green foliage 8 to 15 cm (3 to 6 in.) in height with white or pink flowers in May.

Culture: They do best in light shade in ordinary but well drained soil with even moisture.

Use: Because of their low stature, saxifrages are ideal subjects for the shaded parts of the rock garden.

Propagation: They are most easily propagated by division but can also be grown from seed or cuttings.

Saxifraga sp.

Scabiosa spp.
Scabious or Pincushion Flower

Description: The genus name is from the word scabies, meaning "itch." The plant was once said to cure this dreaded malady. The common name, "pincushion flower," is derived from the fact that the flowers are globe-shaped but have protruding grey stamens which resemble pins.

Scabiosa caucasica (Caucasian scabious) produces delicate, powdery blue or white flowers on 60 cm (2 ft.) stems from mid to late summer. The foliage is dark green and deeply cut.

Scabiosa fischeri (Fischer's scabious) is shorter with smaller flowers and finer leaves.

Scabiosa columbaria (dove scabious) has grey-green leaves and mauve to rose flowers.

Culture: They grow well in a light organic soil which is fertile, reasonably moist, but well-drained and in full sun. They should be divided every 3 or 4 years.

Use: Scabious are excellent for the sunny border and as long-lasting cut flowers.

Propagation: Propagation is by seed, spring division, or basal cuttings.

Scabiosa sp.

Scabiosa sp.

Sedum sp.

Sedum spurium

Sedum spurium 'Dragon's Blood'

Sedum spp.
Stonecrop

Description: The stonecrops form a large group of low succulent plants with both attractive foliage and flowers. Hundreds of species and cultivars are available. The following are among those recommended for the prairie climate:

Sedum ewersii (Ewer's stonecrop) is 30 cm (12 in.) high and has bluish leaves and pink flowers in mid-summer.

Sedum hybridum (evergreen stonecrop) has glossy leaves and yellow flowers in July.

Sedum sieboldii (siebold stonecrop) is 30 cm (12 in.) high with blue-grey leaves and soft pink flowers in July.

Sedum spectabile (showy stonecrop) is a compact plant with upright 30 cm (12 in.) stems and pinky-orange flowers in August. *Sedum spectabile* 'Variegatum' has leaves which are golden variegated.

'Autumn Joy' (*Sedum spectabile* x *S. telephium*) is 60 cm (2 ft.) in height and blooms in September.

Sedum telephium (Japanese sedum) is very similar to 'Autumn Joy', but somewhat tougher under prairie conditions.

Sedum spurium (two-row stonecrop) is a low plant 15 cm (6 in.) high with roundish leaves and pink to red flowers in July. It makes an excellent ground cover.

Sedum acre (golddust stonecrop) is only 8 cm (3 in.) high with masses of tiny leaves and tiny yellow flowers. It spreads quickly and is better used as a ground cover than in a rock garden.

Sedum kamtschaticum (orange stonecrop) has light green leaves and orange yellow flowers on 15 cm (6 in.) stems in July.

Culture: Stonecrops require well-drained soil in full sun. The flowers may be sheared off for a neater appearance once they have faded.

Use: They are well suited to the rock garden or as a ground cover in hot, dry locations.

Propagation: They are easily propagated by stem cuttings or division.

PERENNIALS FOR THE PLAINS AND PRAIRIES

Sempervivum **spp.**
Hens and Chicks or House Leek

Description: Valued primarily for their foliage, hens and chicks consist of succulent leaves arranged in low rosettes with flower stalks occasionally arising from the center. The inflorescence produced in mid-summer is a weird, umbrella-shaped structure with small flowers. The central rosette ("the hen") dies after flowering. "Chicks" or small off-shoots develop around the mother hen. These will mature into hens over the growing season. There are hundreds of cultivars available with a great range of foliage, form and color. Flowers are usually white, cream, or pink. The foliage is seldom over a few centimetres in height although the flower stalks may be up to 30 cm (12 in.).

In Europe, house leeks are often found growing on the tiled roofs of rural homes where they were once thought to prevent fires and strikes of lightning.

Culture: Hens and chicks are drought tolerant, requiring full sun and well-drained soil.

Use: They are ideal subjects for the rockery, for dry areas, or for edging.

Propagation: Although they can be propagated by seed, simply transplanting the chicks is the easiest method of propagation.

Sempervivum regina-amaliae

Sempervivum tectorum

Silene vulgaris maritima
Sea Campion

Description: Sea campion forms a soft, silvery green mound 15 cm (6 in.) in height composed of tiny leaves on trailing stems. It is covered by masses of white flowers with notched petals from June to October. A double-flowered form is also available. Although individual plants are not long-lived, the planting as a whole is perpetuated through self-seeding.

Culture: Sea campions prefer a sunny, well-drained location and are quite tolerant of heat and drought.

Silene vulgaris maritima

Use: They are useful for naturalizing in areas which cannot be irrigated. If seedlings are not controlled, they can over-run a rock garden.

Propagation: Propagation is by seed.

Silene vulgaris

Solidago canadensis

Solidago canadensis

Solidago canadensis x **'Golden Wings'**
Goldenrod

Description: Well known as a wild flower, this garden hybrid is 150 cm (5 ft.) in height with plumes of golden flowers in late summer and fall. Named cultivars including 'Cloth of Gold', 'Crown of Rays', 'Lauren' and 'Peter Pan' are available and worthy of trial. Further testing is needed.

Contrary to popular belief, the pollen of goldenrod is heavy, insect-borne, and not the culprit responsible for hay-fever. (The real villain is ragweed which blooms at the same time.)

Culture: They do well in full sun or partial shade and ordinary soil.

Use: Goldenrod is useful in the back of a large border or naturalized in a meadow garden. The flowers are used as a yellow dye and in arrangements.

Propagation: They are easily propagated by seed or division.

Stachys grandiflora (S. macrantha)
Big Betony

Description: An old-fashioned border plant, betony has whorls of purple flowers in early summer above 45 cm (18 in.) mounds of narrow, heart-shaped, wrinkled leaves with scalloped edges. The flowers are attractive to bees.

Culture: They do well in full sun or partial shade in ordinary soil. They will be more robust if the soil is evenly moist.

Use: Betony is a good subject for the front of the border, a large rock garden, or a cottage garden.

Propagation: They may be propagated by seed or spring division.

Stachys grandiflora

Thalictrum spp
Meadowrue

Description: *Thalictrum aquilegifolium* (columbine meadowrue) has finely cut leaves which closely resemble that of the columbine. The flowers are fluffy panicles of mauve, white, or purple borne in spring or early summer on 60 to 90 cm (2 to 3 ft.) stems. The flowers are dioecious, meaning that male and female flowers are borne on separate plants. Differences will be seen among seed-grown plants as the male flowers are somewhat showier.

Thalictrum speciosissimum or *T. glaucum* (dusty meadowrue) is 60 to 90 cm (2 to 3 ft.) in height with blue-grey leaves and fragrant, creamy yellow flowers.

Thalictrum minus (low meadowrue) is only 38 cm (15 in.) in height, and has rather insignificant yellow-green flowers. It is grown for its foliage which is reminiscent of the houseplant, maidenhair fern.

Culture: All of these grow well in full sun or partial shade in soil which is rich in organic matter and evenly moist.

Thalictrum

Ed Toop

Thalictrum

Use: The taller types are well suited to the back of the perennial border. Both the flowers and foliage are excellent in bouquets. Meadowrues may also be naturalized in the shaded wild garden or used as waterside plantings by streams or ponds.

Propagation: Propagation is by division. They naturalize readily under shady, moist conditions.

Thermopsis sp.

Thermopsis spp.
False Lupine

Description: Where it is difficult to grow lupines, false lupine may be an acceptable substitute. *Thermopsis montana* (mountain thermopsis) is 60 cm (2 ft.) high with spikes of pale yellow flowers in June. The Carolina thermopsis *(T. caroliniana) (T. villosa)* is similar, but 120 cm (4 ft.) in height with blue-green leaves and 30 cm (1 ft.) flower spikes in July. Both have compound leaves.

Culture: False lupine does well in full sun or partial shade. It prefers a well-drained, somewhat sandy soil. Because they are legumes and have the ability to "fix" nitrogen, they do well in soils of low fertility. Once established, they are drought tolerant. After flowering, the foliage sometimes becomes unattractive and may be cut back.

Use: False lupine is well placed in a larger border where taller, yellow plants are uncommon. They go well with delphiniums. They are also useful as cut flowers, but should not be cut until the bottom flowers are open.

Propagation: Propagation is by spring division or seed. Due to a taproot, divisions may require careful aftercare in order to survive. Fresh seed sown outdoors in the fall will germinate in the spring. Older seed will require freezing for a few weeks prior to sowing. Soaking the seeds in warm water or filing the hard seed coats is also recommended.

PERENNIALS FOR THE PLAINS AND PRAIRIES

Thymus spp.
Thyme

Description: Mother-of-thyme (*Thymus serpyllum*) forms a mat of dark-green aromatic foliage 15 cm (6 in.) in height covered with small purple flowers. 'Album' has white flowers. Woolly thyme (*T. pseudolanuginosus*, *T. lanuginosus* or *T. serpyllum lanuginosus*) is only 5 cm (2 in.) high with grey, pubescent leaves and pink flowers. Lemon thyme (*T. x citriodorus*) is 15 cm (6 in.) high with rose flowers and lemon-scented leaves. It will do better in a more sheltered location. 'Aureus' has golden variegated leaves but needs a sheltered location. All of these flower in mid-summer. There appears to be some confusion in names within the nursery trade.

Culture: Thyme demands a well-drained soil and full sun. Adequate snow cover is helpful in that the leaves are evergreen and may desiccate and turn brown if exposed to drying winter winds.

Use: They are an excellent plant in the rock garden, edging a path or patio, between paving stones, as a ground cover, or used as a culinary herb.

Propagation: Propagation is by seed, division, or cuttings.

Thymus serpyllum

Thymus x *citriodorus*

Tradescantia virginiana
(*T. x andersonianna*)
Virginia Spiderwort

Description: The spiderwort is characterized by grassy foliage of 40 to 60 cm (18 to 24 in.), and blue, purple, or red flowers with 3 distinctive petals blooming in mid-summer. Like the daylily, there are numerous buds, but each flower remains open for only one day. Although there is some confusion in the nomenclature, the hybrids sold in nurseries usually have somewhat larger flowers than the native species.

Culture: They do well in full sun or partial shade and in an organic, evenly moist but well-drained soil. Fewer flowers are produced under shaded conditions. Division is needed

Tradescantia virginiana

Tradescantia virginiana

every 3 or 4 years. The foliage can be somewhat sprawly by mid-summer and a light shearing is sometimes recommended.

Use: They make good border plants if planted in diagonal drifts so that the untidy foliage of late summer can be hidden by other plants. They are also useful for naturalizing in moist, shaded areas.

Propagation: Propagation is by seed, spring division, or cuttings taken in summer.

Trollius ledebourii

Trollius ledebourii

Trollius spp.
Globeflower

Description: The globeflower has large, single or double, waxy, buttercup-like flowers in yellow and orange borne on 60 cm (2 ft.) stems in June. Although the outer petals are globe-shaped, the inner ones are narrow and more stamen-like. The leaves are dark green and deeply lobed. Of the globeflowers tested, only *Trollius ledebourii*, a native of Siberia, proved reliably hardy. 'Golden Queen' is a cultivar which is 90 cm (3 ft.) in height. Several cultivars of the European globeflower (*T. europaeus*) have been successfully grown. 'Lemon Queen', with pale yellow flowers, is probably the most extensively grown.

Culture: Globeflowers prefer an organic, evenly moist soil in full or partial shade. Grow them in full sun if moisture is plentiful. Clumps may be left undisturbed for many years.

Use: The globeflowers are striking plants for the shaded border, for naturalizing in a woodland garden, or for waterside plantings. They also make long-lasting cut flowers.

Propagation: Propagation is by division after flowering. They are difficult to grow by seed which should be sown as soon as it is ripe and may take up to a year to break dormancy . Older seed should be frozen prior to sowing.

Valeriana officinalis
Valerian or Garden Heliotrope

Description: An old-fashioned perennial, the valerian or garden heliotrope is 60 to 90 cm (2 to 3 ft.) in height with loose clusters of tiny, white, lightly fragrant flowers in July.

Culture: It grows well in sun or partial shade in ordinary soil.

Use: Valerian is suited to the back of the border, a fragrance garden, or as an accent plant. It may also be naturalized in a woodland setting or in a moist, shaded area.

Propagation: Propagation is by seed or division. It may self-sow.

Valeriana officinalis

Valeriana officinalis

Verbascum spp.
Mullein

Description: *Verbascum nigrum* (dark mullein) is about 90 cm (3 ft.) in height with tall spikes of yellow flowers with purple anthers. It blooms in July and August. Individual plants tend to be short-lived and almost biennial in nature, but they self-seed sufficiently to be a permanent feature of the border. *Verbascum phoeniceum* (purple mullein) is similar with white, pink, rose, or purple flowers.

Culture: Mulleins do best in full sun and well-drained soil.

Verbascum nigrum

Verbascum nigrum

Use: They are a good perennial for the mid-range or back of the perennial border. Yellow flowers are not often found among plants of the height range of the dark mullein.

Propagation: Verbascums are easily propagated by seed or root cuttings.

Veronica spp.
Speedwell

Introduction: A large group of perennials, speedwells vary in height from those which are almost prostrate to about 90 cm (3 ft.). Flower colors range from blue and purple to pink and white. Seed of most veronicas will show considerable variation so vegetative propagation is recommended.

The common name "Speedwell" is confusing in its origin. One source dates the name to the reputed recovery rates that occurred with its early medicinal use. Another refers to its ability to act quickly as a ground cover. A third states the name is from the ship "Speedwell" which accompanied the "Mayflower" to America, but was forced to turn back when it became unseaworthy. The name *Veronica* is associated with St. Veronica who is said to have wiped the brow of Christ on the cross.

Dwarf Speedwells

Description: *Veronica pectinata* (comb speedwell) forms a prostrate grey mat of 5 cm (2 in.) with tiny, white-centered blue or rose flowers in June or July. It roots at stem nodes as it spreads. This is indeed a "cushion plant". It has been reported that a German Shepherd used a 120 cm (4 ft.) spread of it as a very comfortable cushion for the duration of an entire winter. No harm was done to either the friendly shepherd or the speedwell.

Veronica repens (creeping speedwell) is a very dwarf, mat-forming plant of 5 to 10 cm (2 to 4 in.) with pale blue flowers in late June and July. It may suffer dieback where snow cover is inadequate. It also seems to fare better when shaded from the hot summer sun. Rated as "tender" in prairie Canada, it is best attempted only in sheltered locations.

Veronica sp. (dwarf)

Veronica teucrium 'Trehane' [(Hungarian trehane speedwell) variously recorded as a cultivar of *V. prostrata*, *V. latafolia* or *V. teucrium*] is 20 to 30 cm (8 to 12 in.) in height with bright blue flowers in June and July above contrasting golden foliage. It will grow in full sun or partial shade.

Use: These dwarf speedwells are excellent for the rock garden. All do well in full sun and well-drained soil and seem quite drought tolerant.

Propagation: Propagation of most of these is by division, terminal stem cuttings, or seed.

Veronica incana
Woolly Speedwell

Description: The woolly speedwell (*V. incana*) is 30 to 45 cm (12 to 18 in.) in height with grey leaves and spikes of violet blue flowers in July.

Culture: It is fairly drought tolerant and does well in full sun or partial shade in well-drained soil.

Use: The woolly speedwell is a good plant for the rockery, for edging, for the front of the border or as groundcover. It is valuable for its soft grey foliage alone.

Propagation: Propagation is by division or seed.

Gail Rankin

Veronica incana

University of Alberta Plant Science Collection

Veronica repens

Veronica spicata

Veronica spicata

Gail Rankin

Alberta Horticultural Association

Veronica spicata
Spike Speedwell

Description: *Veronica spicata* (spike speedwell) forms a blue spike 45 to 90 cm (18 to 36 in.) in height blooming in July. 'Alba' is a white form of about the same height while 'Rosea' is pink but only 38 cm (15 in.) in height. *Veronica spuria* (bastard speedwell) is similar but shorter, in blue or pink.

Culture: These taller speedwells do best in full sun in well-drained but evenly moist soil.

Use: Excellent as border plants, they are also used as cut flowers.

Propagation: Propagation is by division, stem cuttings, or seed.

Vinca herbacea

Alberta Horticultural Association

Vinca herbacea
Herbaceous Periwinkle

Description: The herbaceous periwinkle (*Vinca herbacea*) has dark green, shiny leaves on 15 cm (6 in.) trailing stems with purple flowers in July.

Culture: It is considered only of medium hardiness and should best be grown in sheltered locations with adequate snow cover. It will do best in partial shade and even moisture.

Use: Where it survives it is excellent as a groundcover, for edging, or in a shaded portion of the rock garden.

Propagation: Propagation is by division or stem cuttings.

Note: the common periwinkle (*V. minor*) is not considered hardy except in sheltered locations with good snow cover.

Vinca herbacea

Viola canadensis
Canada Violet

Description: The word *violet* is from the Latin "via" meaning road or way – thus appropriately implying flowers found along the way.

The Canada violet or western Canada violet (*V. canadensis* or *V. canadensis* var *rugulosa*) is a native plant of 25 to 38 cm (10 to 15 in.) with 1.5 cm (0.5 in.) white flowers with pink veins in late spring and early summer. The leaves are heart-shaped.

Culture: It does well in shade in ordinary or evenly moist soil.

Use: Useful for naturalizing in shaded, woodland areas, it spreads rapidly by means of underground stolons. It is not recommended for the border or rockery because of its aggressive nature.

Propagation: It is easily propagated by underground stolons (rhizomes).

Viola canadensis

Viola pedatifida

Viola pedatifida
Crows Foot Violet

Description: *Viola pedatifida* (crows foot violet) has deeply cut leaves resembling the foot of a crow with violet-blue flowers on 10 cm (4 in.) stems in June and July.

Culture: It seems equally at home in sun or partial shade as long as the soil is well-drained.

Use: It is a good plant for the rockery.

Propagation: Propagation is by seed. It will also self-seed but never to the point of being a nuisance.

Two other violets worth growing in prairie gardens are *Viola jooi* (Hungarian violet) , a compact plant of 8 cm (3 in.) with fragrant pink flowers in May, and *Viola altaica* (Altai violet) which is 15 cm (6 in.) with yellow flowers in mid and late summer.

Viola cornuta (horned or tufted violet) is not generally considered hardy except in sheltered locations with good snow cover.

Viola tricolor

Viola tricolor
Johnny-Jump-Up

Description: The Johnny-jump-up is 15 to 30 cm (6 to 12 in.) in height with typical pansy coloration and "faces." It is biennial in nature.

Culture: A tough survivor, it will do well under practically any conditions of sun, shade, drought, or moisture.

Use: It is a useful plant for naturalizing, but because of its capacity for self-seeding, do not introduce it into a rock garden or border where it might be difficult to control.

Propagation: It is easily propagated by seed!

PERENNIALS FOR THE PLAINS AND PRAIRIES

Yucca glauca
Small Soapweed or Spanish Bayonet

Description: The small soapweed (*Y. glauca*) has narrow, stiff, grey-green leaves with white margins which are attractive throughout the year. (Because they are sharp-pointed, gardeners should be cautious while weeding nearby!) The flowers are bell-shaped and pendulous, creamy-white in color, and produced on 60 to 90 cm (2 to 3 ft.) stalks in July. Soap was once made from the roots of this plant; hence its common name. *Yucca filamentosa* (Adams' needle) is not reliably hardy in prairie regions.

Culture: Native to the Dakotas, Montana, and southern parts of prairie Canada, soapweed is extremely drought tolerant and does well in a well-drained, sandy loam soil in full sun. In moist or heavy soils, they may rot.

Use: Larger than the majority of rockery plants and quite different in form and texture, it is valued as an accent plant.

Propagation: Soapweed is propagated by seed or crown division of offsets. Seed grown plants may take 4 or more years to reach flowering. The flowers are pollinated by a specific moth without whose presence seed may not be formed.

Yucca glauca

Yucca glauca

Reference charts

Regular perennials

Botanical Name	CULTURE — Soil: Evenly Moist	Ordinary	Dry	Light: Full Sun	Partial Shade	Shade	Propagation: Seed	Division	Stem Cuttings	Root Cuttings	Stolons, Bulbs, Corms, etc.	FLOWER — Color: Inconspicuous	White (Night Garden)	Yellow	Orange	Red	Pink	Purple	Blue	Season of Bloom: Early	Midseason	Late	Cut: Fresh	Dried
Achillea filipendulina		•	•	•			•	•	•					•							•	•	•	•
Achillea millefolium		•	•	•			•	•	•		•		•			•	•				•		•	•
Achillea ptarmica		•	•	•			•	•	•		•		•								•		•	•
Achillea tomentosa		•	•	•				•						•						•				
Aconitum napellus	•			•	•			•										•	•		•		•	
Adonis vernalis		•		•	•			•						•						•				
Aegopodium podograria 'Variegatum'	•	•	•	•	•	•		•				•	•							•	•	•		
Ajuga reptans	•				•	•		•										•	•	•	•			
Althaea rosea (Alcea rosea)		•		•			•						•	•		•	•				•			
Alyssum montana		•	•	•			•		•					•						•				
Anchusa azurea	•			•			•	•		•									•	•				
Anemone pulsatilla (Pulsatilla vulgaris)		•		•			•	•		•						•		•		•				
Anemone sylvestris		•		•	•	•	•	•					•							•				
Antennaria spp.		•	•	•			•	•					•				•			•				
Anthemis tinctoria		•	•	•			•	•						•							•		•	
Aquilegia spp.	•	•		•	•		•	•					•	•		•	•	•	•	•		•		
Arabis spp.		•	•	•			•	•	•				•				•			•				
Arrhenatherum eliatus 'Bulbosium variegatum'		•	•	•	•			•				•								•	•	•		
Artemisia ludoviciana 'Silver King'		•	•	•				•	•			•								•	•	•		•
Artemisia schmidtiana 'Silver Mound'		•	•	•					•			•								•	•	•		
Aruncus dioicus (Aruncus sylvester)	•				•		•	•					•								•			•
Aster spp.		•		•	•		•	•					•				•	•	•	•	•		•	

LANDSCAPE USE / FAULTY HABITS

Height Range						Form				Limitations					Special Features					Faulty Habits				Page No.	Common Name
Mat-like: below 15 cm (5 in.)	Edging: 15-24 cm (5-9 in.)	Foreground: 24-50 cm (9-19 in.)	Middle ground: 50-90 cm (19-35 in.)	Background: 90-120 cm (35-47 in.)	Tall background: 120+ cm (47+ in.)	Spreading	Upright	Border	Rockery	Naturalizing/Dry	Naturalizing/Moist	Groundcover/Understory	Paving Stones/Patio	Requires Sheltered Location	Foliage Prominent	Foliage or Flowers Fragrant	Evergreen	Prominent Seed Pods/Fruit	Native Plant	Shabby after Flowering	Aggressive	Disease/Insect Susceptible	Poisonous		
			●				●	●		●														57	Fernleaf Yarrow
		●					●	●		●									●		●			58	Common Yarrow
		●					●	●		●									●		●			58	Sneezewort
●						●		●	●			●	●											59	Woolly Yarrow
			●				●	●			●												●	60	Monkshood
		●					●	●	●															60	Spring Adonis
	●						●			●	●	●			●						●			61	Bishop's Goutweed
●						●			●			●		●	●		●							62	Carpet Bugleweed
					●		●	●														●		63	Hollyhock
	●					●		●	●				●											74	Mountain Alyssum
			●				●			●														63	Italian Bugloss
	●						●	●	●								●							64	European Pasque Flower
	●						●			●	●													65	Snowdrop Anemone
●								●	●	●							●		●					65	Pussytoes
		●					●	●		●										●				66	Camomile, Golden Margeurite
	●	●	●				●	●	●		●								●	●				67	Columbine
	●					●		●	●				●											68	Rockcress
		●					●			●					●					●				69	Tuberous oatgrass
			●				●			●					●	●			●	●				70	Ghost Plant
		●				●		●	●						●	●								70	Wormwood
				●			●	●										●						71	Goats' Beard
	●	●	●				●	●	●	●									●					72	Aster

Regular perennials

Botanical Name	Evenly Moist	Ordinary	Dry	Full Sun	Partial Shade	Shade	Seed	Division	Stem Cuttings	Root Cuttings	Stolons, Bulbs, Corms, etc.	Inconspicuous	White (Night Garden)	Yellow	Orange	Red	Pink	Purple	Blue	Early	Midseason	Late	Fresh	Dried
Astilbe chinensis 'Pumila'	•				•		•	•			•						•				•	•		
Astilbe thunbergii 'Moerheim'	•				•			•					•								•			
Aurinia saxatilis (Alyssum saxatile)		•	•	•			•		•					•						•				
Bergenia spp.		•		•	•	•	•	•									•			•				
Callianthemum angustifolium	•			•	•		•	•					•							•				
Caltha palustris	•			•	•			•						•						•				
Campanula carpatica	•	•		•	•		•	•					•						•	•				
Campanula cochlearifolia (Campanula pusilla)		•		•	•			•											•	•	•			
Campanula glomerata	•	•		•	•								•					•		•	•			
Campanula persicifolia	•	•		•	•		•	•	•				•						•	•	•			
Centaurea montana		•	•	•	•		•												•	•	•		•	
Cerastium tomentosum		•	•	•			•	•	•				•							•	•	•		
Chrysanthemum coccineum	•	•		•			•	•					•			•	•				•		•	
Chrysanthemum x superbum	•	•	•	•	•		•	•					•								•		•	
Chrysanthemum morifolium	•	•		•				•	•				•	•	•	•	•	•				•	•	
Cimicifuga racemosa	•			•	•		•	•					•								•	•		
Clematis integrifolia	•	•		•	•			•	•										•	•				
Clematis recta		•		•			•	•	•				•							•				
Convallaria majalis	•	•			•	•		•					•							•			•	
Corydalis nobilis		•	•	•	•		•							•						•				
Delphinium spp.	•			•			•	•	•				•				•	•	•	•	•		•	
Dianthus barbatus	•	•		•			•						•			•	•			•	•	•		

LANDSCAPE USE — **FAULTY HABITS**

Groupings: *Height Range* = columns Mat-like … Tall background; *Form* = Spreading, Upright; *Limitations* = Border … Requires Sheltered Location; *Special Features* = Foliage Prominent … Native Plant (plus Shabby after Flowering, Aggressive); *Faulty Habits* = Disease/Insect Susceptible, Poisonous.

Mat-like: below 15 cm (5 in.)	Edging: 15-24 cm (5-9 in.)	Foreground: 24-50 cm (9-19 in.)	Middle ground: 50-90 cm (19-35 in.)	Background: 90-120 cm (35-47 in.)	Tall background: 120+ cm (47+ in.)	Spreading	Upright	Border	Rockery	Naturalizing/Dry	Naturalizing/Moist	Groundcover/Understory	Paving Stones/Patio	Requires Sheltered Location	Foliage Prominent	Foliage or Flowers Fragrant	Evergreen	Prominent Seed Pods/Fruit	Native Plant	Shabby after Flowering	Aggressive	Disease/Insect Susceptible	Poisonous	Page Number	Common Name
		•				•	•	•			•			•										73	Dwarf Chinese Astilbe
			•			•	•							•										73	Moerheim's Astilbe
		•				•		•	•			•												74	Basket of Gold Perennial Alyssum
		•				•	•	•			•				•		•							75	Bergenia, Giant Rockfoil
	•					•			•															76	Callianthemum
		•				•					•								•					76	Marsh Marigold
	•	•				•		•	•															77	Bellflower
•						•			•	•	•	•	•								•			78	Creeping Bellflower
		•				•	•				•										•			79	Clustered Bellflower, Danesblood Bellflower
		•					•	•																79	Peachleaf Bellflower
		•					•	•																80	Mountain Bluet, Perennial Cornflower
•						•			•	•		•	•		•		•		•		•			80	Snow-in-Summer
	•	•						•	•											•				81	Painted Daisy
		•	•					•	•	•										•				82	Shasta Daisy
		•	•					•	•					•										82	Chrysanthemum
				•		•	•				•													84	Black Snakeroot, Bugbane
		•				•	•											•						84	Solitary Clematis
			•			•	•									•		•						85	Ground Clematis
	•							•		•	•				•	•					•		•	86	Lily-of-the-Valley
		•				•		•	•	•	•													86	Siberian Corydalis
		•	•	•		•	•															•		87	Delphinium
	•	•				•	•									•	•							88	Sweet William

Regular perennials

Botanical Name	Evenly Moist	Ordinary	Dry	Full Sun	Partial Shade	Shade	Seed	Division	Stem Cuttings	Root Cuttings	Stolons, Bulbs, Corms, etc.	Inconspicuous	White (Night Garden)	Yellow	Orange	Red	Pink	Purple	Blue	Early	Midseason	Late	Fresh	Dried
Dianthus deltoides		•	•	•			•	•									•				•			
Dianthus plumarius		•		•			•		•				•				•			•			•	
Dicentra eximia	•	•			•		•	•	•	•							•			•	•	•		
Dicentra spectabilis	•				•		•	•		•							•			•				
Dictamnus albus (Dictamnus fraxinella)		•		•			•						•				•				•			
Digitalis grandiflora (Digitalis ambigua)	•				•		•							•							•		•	
Doronicum caucasicum (Doronicum cordatum)	•	•			•		•	•						•						•			•	
Draba aizoon (Draba lasiocarpa)		•	•	•				•						•						•				
Dracocephalum grandiflorum	•	•		•	•			•											•	•				
Dryas octopetala		•	•	•			•		•				•							•				
Duchesnea indica		•	•	•	•						•			•						•				
Echinops ritro (Echinops exalatus)		•	•	•			•	•		•									•			•		•
Erigeron speciosus		•		•			•	•	•								•	•	•	•			•	
Eryngium spp.		•	•	•			•	•		•									•	•	•		•	•
Erysimum asperum (Cherianthus allioni)		•		•	•		•								•					•				
Euphorbia cyparissias		•	•	•			•	•	•					•						•				
Festuca ovina var. glauca		•	•	•	•		•	•				•								•	•	•		
Filipendula spp.	•	•				•	•	•					•				•				•		•	
Gaillardia aristata		•	•	•			•	•		•				•	•	•					•	•	•	
Gentiana spp.	•				•	•	•	•											•	•	•	•		
Geranium spp.		•		•	•		•	•	•	•			•				•	•	•	•				
Geum spp.		•		•				•	•					•	•	•				•				

LANDSCAPE USE / FAULTY HABITS

Height Range						Form		Limitations							Special Features						Faulty Habits			Page Number	Common Name
Mat-like: below 15 cm (5 in.)	Edging: 15-24 cm (5-9 in.)	Foreground: 24-50 cm (9-19 in.)	Middle ground: 50-90 cm (19-35 in.)	Background: 90-120 cm (35-47 in.)	Tall background: 120+ cm (47+ in.)	Spreading	Upright	Border	Rockery	Naturalizing/Dry	Naturalizing/Moist	Groundcover/Understory	Paving Stones/Patio	Requires Sheltered Location	Foliage Prominent	Foliage or Flowers Fragrant	Evergreen	Prominent Seed Pods/Fruit	Native Plant	Shabby after Flowering	Aggressive	Disease/Insect Susceptible	Poisonous		
•						•		•	•		•	•	•				•			•				89	Maiden Pink
		•				•		•	•					•	•	•	•							89	Grass Pink
		•					•	•	•															90	Plume Bleeding Heart
			•				•	•	•										•					91	Common Bleeding Heart
			•				•	•	•														•	91	Gasplant, Dittany
			•				•	•	•		•			•									•	92	Yellow Foxglove
		•						•	•															93	Leopardsbane
•						•			•			•					•							93	Aizoon
	•					•			•															94	Dragonhead
•						•			•						•		•		•					94	Mountain Avens
•						•			•		•	•	•	•				•						95	Mock-Strawberry
			•				•		•					•										95	Small Globe Thistle
		•	•			•		•	•										•					96	Oregon Fleabane
			•			•	•		•					•										97	Sea Holly
		•				•		•	•		•						•							97	Siberian Wallflower
		•					•			•		•							•		•		•	98	Cypress Spurge
	•					•		•	•			•		•			•							99	Sheep's Fescue
			•	•		•	•				•													99	Meadowsweet
		•	•			•		•	•	•									•					100	Blanket Flower
	•	•				•		•	•								•		•					101	Gentian
		•	•			•		•	•	•		•												102	Cranesbill Geranium
		•				•	•	•	•															104	Avens

Regular perennials

Botanical Name	Evenly Moist	Ordinary	Dry	Full Sun	Partial Shade	Shade	Seed	Division	Stem Cuttings	Root Cuttings	Stolons, Bulbs, Corms, etc.	Inconspicuous	White (Night Garden)	Yellow	Orange	Red	Pink	Purple	Blue	Early	Midseason	Late	Fresh	Dried
Glechoma hederacea variegata (Nepeta hederacea)		•		•	•			•											•	•	•	•		
Gypsophila paniculata		•	•	•			•		•				•				•				•	•	•	•
Gypsophila repens		•	•	•			•		•				•				•				•			
Heliopsis scabra (Heliopsis helianthoides scabra)	•	•		•	•		•	•	•					•							•	•		
Hemerocallis spp.	•	•	•	•	•	•	•	•						•	•	•	•			•	•	•		
Heuchera spp.		•	•	•				•								•					•		•	
Hosta spp.	•				•	•	•	•					•				•		•	•	•	•		
Iberis sempervirens		•		•			•		•	•			•							•				
Inula ensifolia	•	•		•	•		•	•						•								•		
Iris x *germanica* and hybrids		•		•			•	•					•	•	•	•	•	•	•		•		•	
Iris pseudocorus	•	•	•	•				•						•						•			•	
Iris sibirica	•			•	•		•	•					•					•	•	•			•	
Lamiastrum galeobdolan var. variegatum (L. galeobdolan)		•			•			•	•					•						•	•	•		
Lamium maculatum 'Beacon Silver'	•				•	•		•	•				•				•	•		•	•	•		
Leontopodium alpinum		•		•	•		•	•					•								•			
Liatris spp.		•		•			•	•									•	•			•		•	•
Ligularia dentata	•				•	•	•	•	•					•	•						•			
Limonium spp.	•	•		•			•			•									•		•	•	•	•
Linum spp.		•		•			•		•				•	•					•	•	•	•		
Lychnis arkwrightii	•	•		•	•		•	•							•						•		•	
Lychnis chalcedonica	•	•		•	•		•	•								•					•		•	
Lychnis coronaria		•		•			•									•					•			

LANDSCAPE USE — Height Range · Form · Limitations · Special Features | **FAULTY HABITS**

Mat-like: below 15 cm (5 in.)	Edging: 15-24 cm (5-9 in.)	Foreground: 24-50 cm (9-19 in.)	Middle ground: 50-90 cm (19-35 in.)	Background: 90-120 cm (35-47 in.)	Tall background: 120+ cm (47+ in.)	Spreading	Upright	Border	Rockery	Naturalizing/Dry	Naturalizing/Moist	Groundcover/Understory	Paving Stones/Patio	Requires Sheltered Location	Foliage Prominent	Foliage or Flowers Fragrant	Evergreen	Prominent Seed Pods/Fruit	Native Plant	Shabby after Flowering	Aggressive	Disease/Insect Susceptible	Poisonous	Page Number	Common Name
•						•		•	•			•	•	•					•					104	Variegated Creeping Charlie
			•				•	•		•									•		•			105	Babysbreath
	•					•		•	•	•														106	Creeping Babysbreath
			•				•	•											•					107	Rough Heliopsis
			•	•			•	•		•	•				•	•								107	Daylily
		•					•	•	•		•				•									108	Coral Bells, Alumroot
	•	•	•				•	•	•			•	•		•	•								109	Plantain Lily, Funkia
		•				•		•	•			•	•				•							110	Perennial Candytuft
		•						•	•			•												111	Swordleaf Inula
•	•	•	•	•			•	•							•									112	Bearded Iris
		•					•	•			•				•						•			114	Yellowflag Iris
		•	•				•	•							•									115	Siberian Iris
		•				•						•	•	•	•						•			116	Deadnettle, Yellow Archangel
		•				•						•	•		•									116	Spotted Deadnettle
	•							•	•						•									117	Alpine Edelweiss
			•				•	•											•					118	Gayfeather, Blazing Star
			•				•	•			•													118	Ligularia, Elephant Ears
		•					•	•											•					119	Sea Lavender, Statice
		•	•				•	•	•	•														120	Perennial Flax
		•					•	•						•										121	Arkwright's Campion
		•					•	•			•													121	Maltese Cross
		•					•	•			•				•									122	Rose Campion

Regular perennials

	CULTURE											FLOWER												
	Soil			Light			Propagation					Color								Season of Bloom			Cut	
Botanical Name	Evenly Moist	Ordinary	Dry	Full Sun	Partial Shade	Shade	Seed	Division	Stem Cuttings	Root Cuttings	Stolons, Bulbs, Corms, etc.	Inconspicuous	White (Night Garden)	Yellow	Orange	Red	Pink	Purple	Blue	Early	Midseason	Late	Fresh	Dried
Lychnis haageana	•	•		•	•		•	•							•						•			
Lychnis viscaria 'Splendens Flore-pleno'		•		•				•								•					•		•	
Lysimachia nummularia	•	•		•	•	•		•	•					•						•	•			
Lythrum spp.	•	•		•	•			•										•			•		•	
Malva moschata		•		•			•	•									•				•			
Matteuccia struthiopteris pensylvanica	•					•		•				•								•	•	•		
Mertensia virginica	•	•			•	•	•	•											•	•				
Monarda spp.		•	•	•				•								•	•				•		•	
Myosotis sylvatica	•	•			•	•	•												•	•	•		•	
Nepeta x *ucranica* 'Dropmore'		•		•	•			•	•									•	•		•		•	
Oenothera missouriensis		•	•	•			•							•							•			
Opuntia polyacantha			•	•			•		•					•							•			
Paeonia spp.		•	•	•			•	•					•			•	•			•			•	
Papaver nudicaule		•	•	•			•						•	•	•	•				•	•	•		
Papaver orientale		•		•				•	•	•					•	•					•		•	
Penstemon spp.		•	•	•			•	•	•							•	•	•	•		•		•	
Phalaris arundinacea var. *picta*		•	•	•	•			•				•								•	•			
Phlox spp.		•	•	•				•	•							•	•		•	•				
Phlox carolina	•	•		•				•	•								•				•	•	•	
Physalis alkekengi	•	•		•	•		•	•							•	•						•	•	•
Physostegia virginiana		•		•	•		•	•									•				•	•		
Platycodon grandiflorum		•		•	•		•	•									•		•		•	•	•	

174

Columns are grouped as follows — **LANDSCAPE USE** → Height Range (Mat-like: below 15 cm / 5 in.; Edging: 15–24 cm / 5–9 in.; Foreground: 24–50 cm / 9–19 in.; Middle ground: 50–90 cm / 19–35 in.; Background: 90–120 cm / 35–47 in.; Tall background: 120+ cm / 47+ in.), Form (Spreading; Upright), Limitations (Border; Rockery; Naturalizing/Dry; Naturalizing/Moist; Groundcover/Understory; Paving Stones/Patio; Requires Sheltered Location), Special Features (Foliage Prominent; Foliage or Flowers Fragrant; Evergreen; Prominent Seed Pods/Fruit; Native Plant) — and **FAULTY HABITS** (Shabby after Flowering; Aggressive; Disease/Insect Susceptible; Poisonous).

Mat-like	Edging	Foreground	Middle ground	Background	Tall background	Spreading	Upright	Border	Rockery	Natur./Dry	Natur./Moist	Groundcover/Understory	Paving Stones/Patio	Requires Sheltered Loc.	Foliage Prominent	Foliage/Flowers Fragrant	Evergreen	Prominent Seed Pods/Fruit	Native Plant	Shabby after Flowering	Aggressive	Disease/Insect Susceptible	Poisonous	Page	Common Name
		•				•	•																	121	Haage's Campion
		•				•	•	•																122	
•						•			•		•	•	•								•			123	Moneywort, Creeping Jenny
		•	•			•	•																	124	Lythrum, Loosestrife
			•			•	•																	125	Musk Mallow
			•			•	•				•	•		•	•				•					125	Ostrich Fern
			•			•		•																126	Virginia Bluebells
			•			•	•				•					•			•			•		126	Bee Balm, Bergamot, Oswego Tea
	•					•		•			•	•							•					127	Forget-Me-Not
		•				•	•	•							•	•								128	Catmint
		•				•		•		•														129	Ozark Sundrop, Missouri Evening Primrose
•						•			•	•								•	•					129	Prickly Pear Cactus
			•			•	•									•						•		130	Peony
		•				•	•	•	•										•					131	Iceland Poppy
			•			•	•											•		•				132	Oriental Poppy
	•	•				•				•														133	Beard Tongue
		•	•			•				•	•	•			•						•			134	Ribbon Grass
•						•			•		•		•				•							135	Dwarf Phlox
			•			•	•																	136	Carolina Phlox
			•				•											•			•			136	Chinese Lantern
			•			•	•				•								•		•			137	Obedient Plant, Lion's Heart, False Dragonhead
			•			•	•																	138	Balloonflower

Regular perennials

Botanical Name

Botanical Name	Evenly Moist	Ordinary	Dry	Full Sun	Partial Shade	Shade	Seed	Division	Stem Cuttings	Root Cuttings	Stolons, Bulbs, Corms, etc.	Inconspicuous	White (Night Garden)	Yellow	Orange	Red	Pink	Purple	Blue	Early	Midseason	Late	Fresh	Dried
Polemonium caeruleum	•				•		•	•	•										•		•			
Polygonatum multiflorum	•				•	•	•	•					•							•	•			
Polygonum bistorta	•			•	•		•	•									•			•			•	
Potentilla spp.			•	•			•	•					•	•	•					•				
Primula 'Assiniboine'	•				•			•									•			•				
Primula auricula 'Dusty Miller'	•	•			•		•	•						•		•		•		•				
Primula cortusoides	•				•	•	•	•									•			•				
Primula denticulata	•				•		•	•					•					•		•				
Primula sieboldii	•				•		•						•				•	•						
Pulmonaria spp.	•				•	•	•	•		•							•	•	•	•				
Ranunculus acris var. *flore-pleno*	•	•		•	•		•	•						•							•	•		
Rheum palmatum		•		•	•			•					•		•						•	•		
Rudbeckia laciniata var. *flore-pleno*	•			•				•						•								•	•	
Salvia	•			•			•	•	•			•							•		•		•	•
Sanguinaria canadensis	•				•	•	•	•					•							•				
Saponaria ocymoides		•		•			•	•	•								•			•				
Saxifraga spp.	•	•			•		•	•	•				•			•	•			•				
Scabiosa spp.	•	•		•			•	•	•				•				•		•	•	•	•	•	
Sedum spp.		•	•	•				•						•	•	•	•			•	•	•		
Sempervivum spp.		•	•	•			•	•					•				•			•	•	•		
Silene vulgaris maritima		•	•	•			•						•							•	•	•		
Solidago canadensis x 'Golden Wings'		•		•	•		•	•						•								•	•	•

Mat-like: below 15 cm (5 in.)	Edging: 15-24 cm (5-9 in.)	Foreground: 24-50 cm (9-19 in.)	Middle ground: 50-90 cm (19-35 in.)	Background: 90-120 cm (35-47 in.)	Tall background: 120+ cm (47+ in.)	Spreading	Upright	Border	Rockery	Naturalizing/Dry	Naturalizing/Moist	Groundcover/Understory	Paving Stones/Patio	Requires Sheltered Location	Foliage Prominent	Foliage or Flowers Fragrant	Evergreen	Prominent Seed Pods/Fruit	Native Plant	Shabby after Flowering	Aggressive	Disease/Insect Susceptible	Poisonous	Page Number	Common Name
		•				•		•		•														138	Jacob's Ladder
		•				•		•		•				•				•						139	Eurasian Solomon's Seal
		•								•														140	Knotweed, Fleeceflower
	•	•	•			•		•	•	•	•								•					140	Cinquefoil
	•						•		•															142	Assiniboine Primrose
	•						•		•					•										142	Dusty Miller Primrose
	•						•		•															142	Cortusa Primrose
	•						•		•				•											142	Drumstick or Himalayan Primrose
	•						•		•				•											143	Siebold Primrose
	•						•		•		•			•	•									144	Lungwort
			•				•	•		•														144	Tall Buttercup, Yellow Bachelor's Button
			•				•	•							•								•	145	Oriental Rhubarb, Sorrel Rhubarb
			•				•	•																146	Coneflower, Golden Glow
		•					•	•																146	Sage
	•					•		•	•										•					147	Bloodroot
•						•			•			•	•											148	Rock Soapwort
•						•			•				•	•			•		•					148	Saxifrage
		•					•	•																149	Scabious, Pincushion Flower
•	•	•	•			•	•	•	•	•	•						•		•					150	Stonecrop
•	•					•			•	•		•	•		•		•							151	Hens and Chicks, House Leek
	•					•				•											•			151	Sea Campion
			•				•	•		•									•		•			152	Goldenrod

Regular perennials

CULTURE: Soil · Light · Propagation **FLOWER:** Color · Season of Bloom · Cut

Botanical Name	Evenly Moist	Ordinary	Dry	Full Sun	Partial Shade	Shade	Seed	Division	Stem Cuttings	Root Cuttings	Stolons, Bulbs, Corms, etc.	Inconspicuous	White (Night Garden)	Yellow	Orange	Red	Pink	Purple	Blue	Early	Midseason	Late	Fresh	Dried
Stachys grandiflora (S. macrantha)	•	•		•	•		•	•										•		•				
Thalictrum spp.	•	•		•	•			•					•					•		•	•		•	
Thermopsis spp.		•	•	•	•		•	•						•						•	•		•	
Thymus spp.		•		•			•	•	•				•				•	•		•				
Tradescantia virginiana (T. x andersoniana)	•			•	•		•	•	•						•			•	•	•				
Trollius spp.	•				•	•		•						•	•					•			•	
Valeriana officinalis		•		•	•		•	•					•								•			
Verbascum spp.		•	•	•			•			•			•								•	•		
Veronica spp.	•	•	•	•	•		•	•	•				•				•	•	•	•	•		•	
Veronica incana		•	•	•	•		•	•										•		•				
Veronica spicata	•	•		•			•	•	•				•				•	•		•			•	
Vinca herbacea	•	•			•			•	•									•		•				
Viola canadensis	•	•			•	•					•		•							•				
Viola pedatifida		•		•	•		•											•		•	•	•		
Viola tricolor	•	•	•	•	•	•	•							•				•	•	•	•			
Yucca glauca		•	•	•			•	•					•							•				

Table — LANDSCAPE USE and FAULTY HABITS

Height Range						Form		Limitations							Special Features					Faulty Habits				Page	Common Name
Mat-like: below 15 cm (5 in.)	Edging: 15-24 cm (5-9 in.)	Foreground: 24-50 cm (9-19 in.)	Middle ground: 50-90 cm (19-35 in.)	Background: 90-120 cm (35-47 in.)	Tall background: 120+ cm (47+ in.)	Spreading	Upright	Border	Rockery	Naturalizing/Dry	Naturalizing/Moist	Groundcover/Understory	Paving Stones/Patio	Requires Sheltered Location	Foliage Prominent	Foliage or Flowers Fragrant	Evergreen	Prominent Seed Pods/Fruit	Native Plant	Shabby after Flowering	Aggressive	Disease/Insect Susceptible	Poisonous	Page Number	
		•				•		•	•															153	Big Betony
		•	•				•	•			•													153	Meadowrue
			•	•			•	•																154	False Lupine
•						•		•	•	•		•	•	•	•	•	•							155	Thyme
		•	•				•	•			•								•					155	Virginia Spiderwort
		•					•	•			•													156	Ledebour Globeflower
		•					•	•			•					•								157	Valerian or Garden Heliotrope
		•	•				•	•		•									•					157	Mullein
•	•	•	•			•	•	•	•															158	Speedwell
		•				•	•	•			•				•									159	Woolly Speedwell
		•					•	•																160	Spike Speedwell
•						•					•		•	•										160	Herbaceous Periwinkle
		•				•	•				•	•									•			161	Canada Violet
•							•			•														162	Crow's Foot Violet
	•						•				•	•	•											162	Johnny-Jump-Up
		•					•			•					•			•	•					163	Small Soapweed, Spanish Bayonet

Bulbs

Botanical Name	CULTURE — Soil: Evenly Moist	Ordinary	Dry	Light: Full Sun	Partial Shade	Shade	Propagation: Seed	Division	Stem Cuttings	Root Cuttings	Stolons, Bulbs, Corms, etc.	FLOWER — Color: Inconspicuous	White (Night Garden)	Yellow	Orange	Red	Pink	Purple	Blue	Season of Bloom: Early	Midseason	Late	Cut: Fresh	Dried
Allium caeruleum		•		•			•				•								•	•	•			
Allium moly		•		•			•				•			•						•	•			
Allium neopolitanum		•		•			•				•		•							•				
Allium oreophilum		•		•			•				•						•			•	•			
Allium schoenoprasum		•		•	•		•	•			•						•	•		•	•			
Chionodoxa luciliae		•		•			•				•								•	•				
Crocus spp.		•		•							•		•	•	•			•	•					
Fritillaria meleagris		•		•							•							•		•				
Fritillaria pallidiflora		•		•							•			•						•				
Ixiolirion spp.		•		•							•						•	•		•	•			
Lilium spp. & hybrids	•			•	•		•				•		•	•	•	•	•				•		•	
Muscari spp.		•		•			•				•		•					•	•	•				
Narcissus spp.		•			•		•				•		•	•						•			•	
Puschkinia spp.		•		•			•				•		•							•	•			
Scilla sibirica		•		•			•				•		•							•	•			
Tulipa hybrids		•		•							•		•	•	•	•	•	•		•			•	
Tulipa tarda		•		•							•			•						•				
Tulipa kolpakowskiana		•	•	•							•			•						•				

LANDSCAPE USE																					FAULTY HABITS				
Height Range						Form		Limitations							Special Features										
Mat-like: below 15 cm (5 in.)	Edging: 15-24 cm (5-9 in.)	Foreground: 24-50 cm (9-19 in.)	Middle ground: 50-90 cm (19-35 in.)	Background: 90-120 cm (35-47 in.)	Tall background: 120+ cm (47+ in.)	Spreading	Upright	Border	Rockery	Naturalizing/Dry	Naturalizing/Moist	Groundcover/Understory	Paving Stones/Patio	Requires Sheltered Location	Foliage Prominent	Foliage or Flowers Fragrant	Evergreen	Prominent Seed Pods/Fruit	Native Plant	Shabby after Flowering	Aggressive	Disease/Insect Susceptible	Poisonous	Page Number	Common Name
		•					•	•																44	Blue Globe Onion
		•					•	•	•															44	Golden Garlic
		•					•	•	•					•										44	Naples Onion
•	•							•	•															44	Ostrowsky Onion
		•				•	•	•																43	Chives
•	•					•		•	•	•	•	•							•					42	Glory of the Snow
•							•	•	•		•		•						•					41	Crocus
		•					•	•	•															43	Checkered Lily
	•						•	•	•															43	Siberian Fritillary
		•					•	•	•		•			•										43	Ixiolirion
	•	•	•				•	•	•		•											•		44	Lilies
	•					•	•	•	•		•			•					•					42	Grape Hyacinth
	•	•					•	•	•	•	•	•		•					•					39	Daffodil
•	•					•		•	•	•	•	•							•					42	Striped Squill
•	•					•		•	•	•	•	•							•					42	Squill
		•				•	•	•						•					•					37	Common Garden Tulips
•						•			•	•														39	Tarda Tulip
		•				•	•	•	•										•					39	

PERENNIALS FOR THE PLAINS AND PRAIRIES

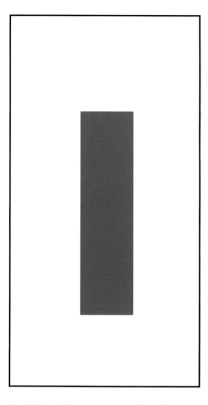

Glossary

Acidity: the amount of acid present (associated with high hydrogen ion concentration). See pH.

Adventitious: said of structures arising from places other than the usual: eg roots growing from leaves or buds developing at locations other than leaf axils (nodes) or shoot apices.

Alkalinity: the amount of hydroxides present (associated with low hydrogen ion concentration). See pH.

Alpine plant: a plant indigenous or native to high elevation mountain meadows or adaptable to such environmental conditions.

Analagous: referring to a flower bed color scheme in which the colors used are adjoining one another on the color wheel. (eg red and red-violet, or orange, yellow-orange and yellow).

Annual: a plant that completes its life cycle within one year. During this time it grows, flowers, produces seeds, and dies.

Axil: the angle formed between a stem and the base of the petiole of a leaf; normally the site of a lateral bud.

Basal rosette: a cluster or whorl of leaves at ground level, typical of the first season vegetative growth of a biennial; a cluster of leaves at the base of a flower stalk.

Biennial: a plant that completes its life cycle within two years, the first season's growth being strictly vegetative.

Birren system: a scheme for outdoor color which uses six primaries listed in a descending order of the amount of light reflected from each: white 80%, yellow 55%, green 35%, red 25%, blue 20%, and black 0%.

Blast: the failure of a flower bud within a bulb to mature into an attractive and functional flower.

Botrytis: a genus of pathogenic fungi that causes disease in various kinds of plants.

Bracts: modified leaves which may occur immediately below a flower or flower head and appear to be part of the flower.

Broken: used in reference to tulip cultivars in which the flowers show variegation in the form of long stripes of white or pale color in the tepals.

Bud sport: a mutation which occurs within a bud causing the shoot which develops from that bud to be genetically different from the rest of the plant.

Bulb: a bud-like plant storage structure, generally globe shaped, composed of fleshy leaf bases attached to a disk-shaped stem plate.

Chroma: the purity of color or hue; its freedom from white, grey or black (tint, tone or shade).

Complementary: referring to a flower bed color scheme in which the colors used are opposite one another on the color wheel (eg yellow and violet or orange and blue)

Compound leaves: leaves which have the usual blade portion divided into individual leaflets.

Corm: an underground storage organ similar to a bulb but consisting of swollen stem tissue covered with dry membranous leaf bases.

Corona: a crown or inner petal-like appendage, as is found in flowers of *Narcissus*.

Crown: the place where stems and roots meet, usually at ground level.

Cultivar: a uniform group of cultivated plants obtained by breeding or selection, and propagated as a pure line; a horticultural or agricultural variety.

Cuttings: leaves, roots, or stems of a plant removed to form roots and other missing parts to propagate a new plant.

Dioecious: refers to individual plants of a given kind having either male (staminate) or female (pistilate) flowers but not both.

Dissect: to cut apart.

Division: to dissect the crown of an herbaceous perennial for purposes of propagation.

Dormancy: lack of growth of seeds, buds, bulbs, etc. due to unfavorable environmental conditions (external dormancy) or to factors within the organ itself (internal dormancy or rest).

Dormant: in a state of inactivity or apparent inactivity.

Drifts: refers to mounds of color of irregular shape and size produced in a flower border as a result of careful planning; informal or natural looking placement of plants within a bed or border.

Embryo: a miniature plant within a seed, normally produced from a zygote as the result of the union of gametes (sperm and egg).

Escape from cultivation: a domesticated plant that has become naturalized in a particular area and is capable of thriving and multiplying on its own (a non-native wild plant).

Essential elements: all the nutrients required, both mineral and non-mineral, for healthy plant growth.

Everlasting: flowers of various plants which retain their shape and color when air dried and are useful for winter bouquets and arrangements, e.g., Statice (*Limonium* spp.).

Fibrous roots: a root system composed of relatively thin roots that branch and rebranch to form an expanding network.

Floret: a small flower; the individual flowers that make up a flower head or inflorescence.

Foundation planting: plants placed to hide the foundation of a house or other building; a planting along a foundation.

Genus (Genera): the usual major subdivision(s) of a family in the classification of plants or animals; each genus usually consists of more than one species.

Germination: the process whereby the embryo in a seed grows and emerges from the seed to become a seedling.

Graft: the joining of two separate structures such as a root and stem or two stems, so that by tissue regeneration they form a union and grow as one plant.

Ground cover: refers to low-growing plants that spread readily to cover the ground with vegetation.

Hardy: refers to plants adapted to cold temperatures or other adverse environmental conditions of an area.

Herbaceous perennial: a plant which lives for three or more growing seasons and does not develop woody tissues.

Hue: color; the colors of the rainbow or refracted white light, e.g., red, yellow, orange, etc.

Hybrid: the offspring of two plants of different genetic makeup.

Imbricate bulb: a bulb composed of many fleshy scales that overlap one another like shingles.

Inflorescence: a collective term for a group of flowers attached to a common axis (stem).

Internodal: referring to the parts of a stem between nodes.

Interplant: to plant one kind of plant in between (an)other kind(s) of plants.

Lanceolate: shaped like a lance-head, several times longer than wide, broadest toward the base and narrowed to the apex.

Layering: a form of vegetative propagation in which an intact stem develops roots as the result of contact with the soil (or another rooting medium).

Legume: a plant belonging to the pulse or pea family (*Leguminosae*).

Linear leaf: a leaf that is long and narrow with parallel margins.

Loam: refers to a soil in which the proportion of sand, silt, and clay are approximately equal.

Lobed: having rounded projections or divisions; in reference to leaves, having lobes or divisions extending less than half way to the middle of the blade.

Luminosity: the quality or condition of radiating or reflecting light.

Macronutrients: those nutrients required by plants in relatively large amounts, eg nitrogen, phosphorus, potassium.

Marginally hardy: on the borderline of being hardy enough to survive in a given climatic zone.

Massed: plants of one kind grouped in quantity close together to produce a strong visual effect.

Microclimate: atmospheric environmental conditions in the immediate vicinity of a plant. It includes interchanges of energy, gases, and water between atmosphere and soil.

Midrib: the central vein of a leaf blade.

Monochromatic: referring to a flower bed color scheme in which the colors used are one hue (eg red) with perhaps some white flowers to strengthen the pastel or pale tints.

Mulch: a material such as straw, leaves, peat, compost, etc., that is spread upon the surface of the soil to protect the soil and plant roots and crowns from the effects of rain, soil crusting, freezing, or evaporation.

Naturalize: to introduce a plant from one environment to another to which the plant becomes established and more or less adapted by surviving for many generations.

Night garden: a garden that is visibly attractive in very low light (night-time conditions) containing white or luminous colored flowers and/or highly reflective foliage (grey or bright green).

Nodes: the regions of stems where leaves are attached and buds are located.

Nomenclature: a set or system of names or terms such as those used in the classification of plants.

Off-shoots: short, horizontal stems which occur in whorls or near whorls in plant crowns.

Opposite leaves: refers to plants which produce two leaves at each node; used as a trait for identification and classification.

Organic matter: carbon containing materials of either plant or animal origin, which exist in all stages of decomposition in soils.

Organic soil: a soil containing a high percentage of organic matter.

Ornamental: refers to a plant grown for its aesthetic properties.

Ovate: egg-shaped: having an outline like that of an egg, with the broader end basal.

Ovoid: a solid with an ovate outline (see ovate).

Palmate: refers to a compound leaf with all the leaflets arising from one point at the end of the petiole. May also refer to the pattern of veins in the blade of a simple leaf.

Panicle: a type of inflorescence similar to a raceme, but with a branched cluster of flowers in place of each single flower of a raceme.

pH: a measure of acidity or alkalinity expressed as the negative log of the hydrogen ion concentration. A pH of 7 is neutral; less than 7 is acidic; more than 7 is basic or alkaline.

Pinnate: refers to a compound leaf with the leaflets arranged along both sides of a common axis. May also refer to the pattern of veins in a simple leaf where secondary veins extend laterally from a single midrib.

Pips: individual pieces of rootstock easily separated for propagation purposes; e.g., lily-of-the-valley.

Propagation: the act of propagating or multiplying by any process of natural reproduction from the parent stock.

Prostrate: a plant or stem of a plant which lies flat on the ground.

Pubescent: covered with short hairs, usually fine or down-like.

Raceme: a type of inflorescence in which stalked flowers are borne on a single, unbranched main axis.

Reflexed: abruptly bent or turned downward.

Rhizome: a horizontal stem that grows partly or entirely underground, often thickened and serving as a storage organ.

Ribbon planting: a narrow bed or planting of flowers along a walkway, wall, fence, or other such structure.

Rosette: a dense cluster of leaves on a very short stem or axis.

Saline soil: an alkali soil with more than 2000 ppm soluble salts, but relatively low sodium content. Such soils can often be reclaimed by leaching.

Scarification: the chemical or physical treatment used on some kinds of seeds in order to break or weaken the seed coat sufficiently for germination to occur.

Self-sow: plants which propagate themselves from seed once established.

Senescence: growing old, aging; the deterioration of plant tissues and their final death.

Separation: the use of bulbs and corms in propagation utilizing the naturally detachable parts.

Sessile: without a petiole (as in some leaves), or without a pedicel (as in some flowers).

Softwood cuttings: cuttings taken from soft, succulent, new spring growth of deciduous or evergreen species of woody plants.

Species: a group of similar distinct plants capable of interbreeding to produce offspring like themselves. One or more species make up a genus.

Specimen plant: a plant placed by itself in the landscape as a focal point or point of interest.

Spike: a type of inflorescence similar to a raceme but having sessile (stalkless) flowers or florets attached directly to the central axis with the oldest flowers at the base.

Spore: a reproductive body, usually a single detached cell without embryo, as in ferns.

Stamen: the male reproductive organ of a plant.

Sterile: infertile; not capable of producing viable seeds.

Stolon: a runner, or any basal branch or above-ground stem that is inclined to root at the nodes when it comes into contact with the ground.

Stratification: the storing of seeds at low temperature of 2 to 4°C (32 to 40°F) usually, under moist conditions in order to break physiological dormancy or rest.

Stratified: placed in strata or layers, seed that has been stored between layers of moist earth or peat moss in order to break dormancy (see stratification).

Subshrub: a plant that is partly woody and partly herbaceous in character, or which becomes woody under certain climatic conditions (generally high temperatures).

Succulent: a plant having fleshy and juicy tissues; non-woody.

Sun scald: high temperature injury to plant tissue due to exposure to intense sunlight.

Systemic: describes a pesticide that acts through a plant's tissues, poisoning a pest that attacks the plant.

Taproot: an elongated, deeply growing primary root.

Tepals: a term used to denote either a sepal or a petal on flowers in which these structures are indistinguishable from one another (e.g., tulip, lily).

Terminal: used in reference to stem cuttings in which only the upper end portion of a plant shoot is used to make the cutting.

Tissue culture: the growing of masses of cells on agar or in liquid suspension from which buds or embryos can be induced to form as a means of rapid asexual multiplication of plants.

True bulbs: plant storage organs that are bulbs, not bulb-like structures (see definition of bulb).

Tuber: an enlarged underground stem tip serving as a storage organ of starch or related materials.

Tuberous root: a thick, tuber-like root which serves as a storage organ.

Turkscap blossoms: refers to lily flowers in which the tepals are recurved toward their point of attachment on the pedicel to give a turban-like appearance to the flower.

Umbel: a type of inflorescence in which the individual flower stalks (pedicels) all arise from the tip of the main stalk (peduncle).

Underplant: to put plants under the canopy of larger taller plants.

Value: refers to the reflectiveness of flower colors. White and yellow are considered high value colors, whereas red and blue are considered low value (see Birren system).

Variegated: patterned with two distinct colors or shades of color. Mostly applied to yellow and green or white and green leaves, but can also apply to flowers.

Vegetative: referring to asexual (stem, leaf, root) development in plants in contrast to sexual (flower, fruit, seed) development.

White garden: a garden consisting of only plants with white flowers and/or plants with grey or silvery foliage.

Whorled cluster: a group of three or more flowers, fruits, leaves, etc., arising from a common point of attachment.

Whorled leaves: a group of three or more leaves arising from the same node.

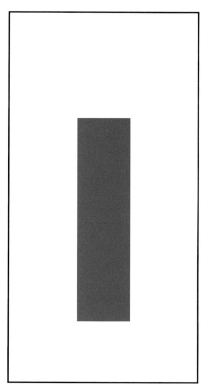

References

Anderson, E G. *Hardy Bulbs I.* Penguin Books, Inc, 1964.

Buckley, A R. *Canadian Garden Perennials.* Hancock House, 1977

Cumming, Roderick W. and Robert E Lee. *Contemporary Perennials.* Macmillan Co.,New York: 1960.

Harp, H F. *Herbaceous Perennials for the Prairies.* Canada Department of Agriculture, 1971

Hortus Third, Cornell University, Macmillan, 1976

Hudak, Joseph. *Gardening with Perennials Month by Month.* New York Times Book Co, 1976.

Perry, Frances. *Complete Guide to Hardy Perennials.* Charles T Bronford Company, Boston, Mass: 1958.

Skinner, F L. *Horticultural Horizons.* Manitoba Department of Agriculture and Conservation, 1966

Wyman, Donald. *Wyman's Gardening Encyclopedia.* Macmillan, 1976

Vance, F R, J R Jowsey, J S McLean. *Wildflowers Across the Prairies.* Western Producer Prairie Books, 1984

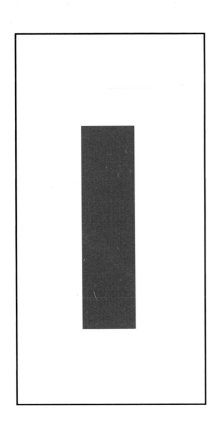

Places to visit

There are undoubtedly many good perennial plantings in public parks throughout the Prairie Provinces, but there are a few well known ones listed below:

Devonian Botanic Garden
University of Alberta
Edmonton, Alberta
T6G 2E9

Alberta Special Crops and Horticulture Research Center
Brooks, Alberta
T0J 0J0

Forestry Farm Park
Attridge Drive and Forestry Farm Road
Saskatoon, Saskatchewan

PFRA Tree Nursery
Indian Head, Saskatchewan
S0G 2K0

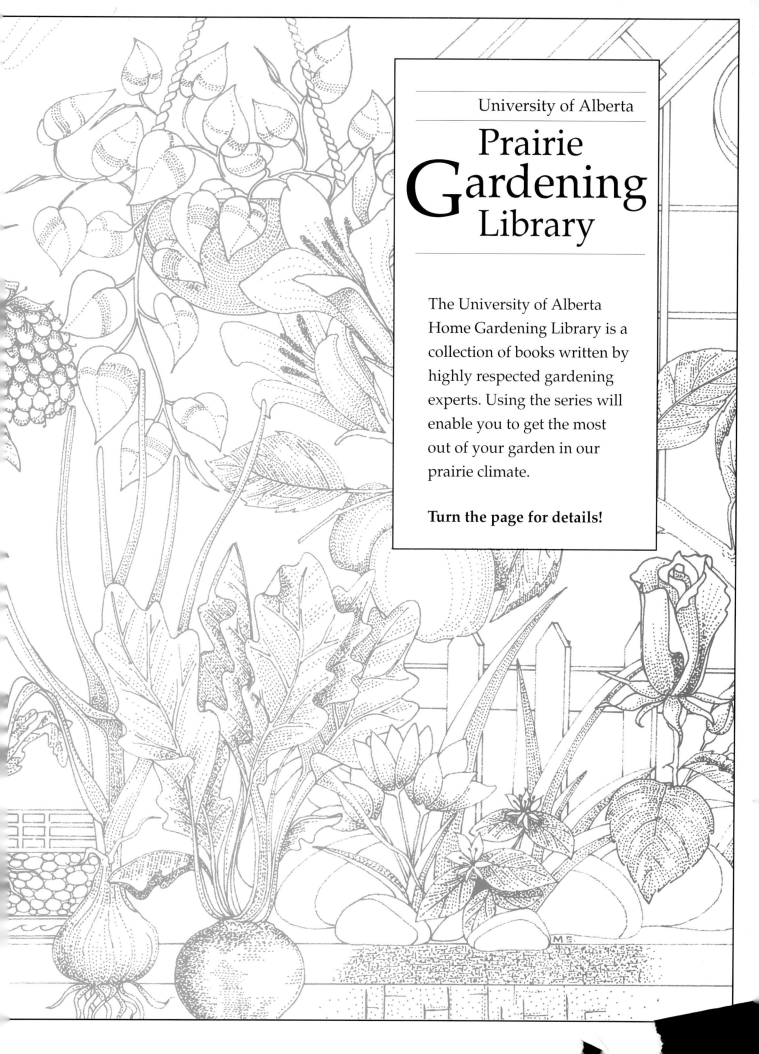

University of Alberta
Prairie
Gardening
Library

The University of Alberta
Home Gardening Library is a
collection of books written by
highly respected gardening
experts. Using the series will
enable you to get the most
out of your garden in our
prairie climate.

Turn the page for details!

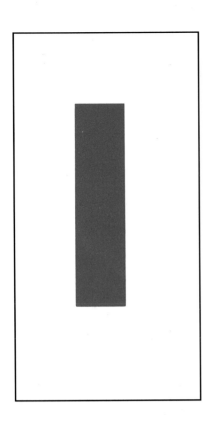

The Prairie Gardening Series

Insect Pests of the Prairies
This is your guide to identification and control of over 220 insects common to the Prairies.

Perennials for the Prairies
This is the ultimate reference book on growing, maintaining, and enjoying perennials suitable for our harsh climate.

Rose Gardening on the Prairies
Take the guesswork out of developing a healthy, vigorous, and productive rose garden.

Woody Ornamentals for the Prairies
More than a list of trees and shrubs, this book contains invaluable information for planting, maintenance, survival, and landscape design.

Annuals for the Prairies
The new standard reference for Prairie gardeners of more than 150 annual specimens suitable for our short growing season, and complete details on how to choose, cultivate and enjoy them.

Home Gardening Course
This is an up-to-date, practical course explaining the why's and how's of gardening for the novice or advanced gardener. Study it systematically as a course or use it as a gardening guide.

Available at your local garden centre, book stores, or order them directly from the University of Alberta.

Use your VISA or MasterCard and phone: (403) 492-9273

      OR write to:

University Bookstore
University Extension Centre
8303 112 Street
Edmonton, Alberta T6G 2T4